Party Fun!

Dedicated to Nicholas and Amy

JENNY DODD

ACKNOWLEDGEMENTS

Without the expertise of the hard-working team at Struik, this book wouldn't have been possible. My special thanks to Linda de Villiers for guiding the ship throughout the journey. To Joy Clack, for her patient and professional editing that turned a wad of text into this fabulous guide for parents – her dedication is apparent throughout! To Beverley Dodd, whose design skills have transformed every page into a fantasy of inspiration – I am delighted to have once again had the opportunity to take advantage of her talents! For the many evenings spent in my kitchen, icing nozzle in hand, I thank you too, Bev. I would never have managed this production without your devoted assistance.

My husband, Cedric, came up trumps and spent many hours patiently waiting outside toy and baking supply stores. He tirelessly helped with my props and contributed much to this project. My 'technical advisers', Nicholas Latimer and Amy Dodd, provided much valued input. We spent many happy hours in our 'design studio' mulling over ideas. Amy was a real asset in the kitchen too as she ably assisted with the cake decorating, managing the tasks delegated to her with aplomb!

My dear friend Kirsten Roets advised with the beading designs and instructions. The many hours spent in bead shops and the subsequent afternoons devoted to transforming fishing line into artworks are much appreciated. Natalie Dodd and Yvonne von Ruben encouraged me all the way and I thank them for their unfailing support and enthusiasm.

Ryno's expertise behind the lens and his keen eye for detail is clearly evident on every page. His professional input did much to enhance my designs. Anke's styling was an absolute joy to behold and fulfilled all my expectations! Ably assisted by Shelley, the party tables are guaranteed to evoke squeals of delight.

Lastly, our two standard poodles were delighted when the food mixer once again started churning in preparation of this book and there was much happy anticipation of reject designs! JENNY DODD

Note: While every effort has been made to ensure that the information contained in this book is accurate, the author and publishers accept no responsibility for any loss, injury or inconvenience sustained by any person using this book or following the advice given in it.

This edition first published in 2007 by
New Holland Publishers (UK) Ltd
Cape Town • London • Sydney • Auckland
www.newhollandpublishers.com

Garfield House, 86–88 Edgware Road, London W2 2EA,
United Kingdom
80 McKenzie Street, Cape Town 8001, South Africa
14 Aquatic Drive, Frenchs Forest, NSW 2086, Australia
218 Lake Road, Northcote, Auckland, New Zealand

ISBN 978 1 84537 915 5

1 2 3 4 5 6 7 8 9 10

PUBLISHING MANAGER: Linda de Villiers
EDITOR: Joy Clack
DESIGNER: Beverley Dodd
PHOTOGRAPHER: Ryno
STYLIST: Anke Roux
ILLUSTRATOR: Janine Damon
PROOFREADER: Irma van Wyk

Reproduction by Hirt & Carter Cape (Pty) Ltd
Printed and bound by Tien Wah Press (Pte) Limited, Singapore

www.imagesofafrica.co.za
IMAGES OF AFRICA
PHOTO LIBRARY

CONTENTS

INTRODUCTION

Children's birthdays are always anticipated with a great deal of excitement and the planning and preparations for this special day can make all the difference to the enjoyment of the occasion. A well-planned party is also long remembered and much appreciated.

It is with all this in mind that I have endeavoured to provide this second guide for children's parties and to show you how to enchant the entire family as they witness flour, icing sugar and sweets being transformed before their eyes. My intent is to illustrate just how easy it is to produce a birthday cake in your own kitchen. Plan ahead, shop around, bake in advance and you will wish that birthdays could be more frequent events on the calendar! The confectionery accessories that are currently available make cake decorating a cinch and sweet manufacturers are providing such a variety of shapes that any theme can easily be co-ordinated.

From the time that the theme is chosen and the guest list prepared, the party will be anticipated with tangible excitement. Involve your child in all the preparations and allow and respect his or her opinions and suggestions.

Record the happy event by taking photographs and include a video as well, if possible. These will provide treasured memories that will last forever!

PARTY PREPARATIONS

The key to a successful party is to plan ahead and make the cake well in advance, not on the day of the party! Once the cake has been iced it may be covered with a large plastic bag and frozen until the day before the party, when the finishing touches may be added. Cupcakes and biscuits may also be made in advance and frozen, again adding the final decorations on the day before the party.

PARTY THEMES

The themes depicted in this book can be achieved relatively quickly and easily and at a low cost, but they can all be adapted to suit time and budget constraints. Many of the ideas are interchangeable, for example the beading activities will also work very well with the girls' sleepover party. Babies and toddlers have been included in this book and I trust that the theme ideas will be of assistance, especially to first-time mums!

PARTY DÉCOR

Setting the scene for the party need not be a formidable chore, especially if planned in advance. Involve the entire family in creating the items that contribute to the enchantment of the chosen theme. Not only is this a good way to spend time together, it will also speed up the preparations if you're pushed for time.

Streamers (50 mm wide) cut from sheets of crepe paper are easy to make and, when twisted before hanging, create a wonderful canopy above the party table that can reflect the dominant colours of the theme. Use a pair of pinking scissors when cutting the streamers to add to the effect and staple the ends of the streamers together to increase the length if necessary.

Balloons always add extra appeal to any party atmosphere. It has become standard practice to tie a bunch to the garden gate, allowing easy identification of the party venue and letting the neighbourhood know that a very special day is being celebrated. Tie balloons in bunches (the theme will determine the colours) in the corners of the party room and wherever else the children are likely to gather. Add curling ribbons to enhance the festive appearance. Dispose of broken bits of balloon immediately as they may be dangerous if swallowed. Tips for décor have been included with each theme.

INVITATIONS

Invitations should be distributed about two weeks before the party. Always include an RSVP date to facilitate catering as well as the preparation of the games – contact the mums who haven't replied to ascertain whether their child will be accepting the invitation. Give the birthday child the guest list so that he or she may tick off the names as the replies are received.

Apart from the starting time, stipulate the time that the party will end so that parents collect the children punctually. Ensure that the duration of the party is not too long – two hours is sufficient for most parties. Parties for babies and toddlers may be restricted to 1½ hours, while those for the older children that involve outings, for example the skateboarding and tenpin bowling, will need to be quite a bit longer. Always ensure that you have a contact number for the parents of each guest.

The invitation provides a foretaste of the party so try to be original and creative and incorporate party favours where possible. I have included invitations to complement each theme with easy step-by-step instructions for how to put them together, plus ideas for the wording of the invitation details. I have tried to keep the invitations simple, yet appealing, so that the birthday child may assist in making them. If time is limited, ready-made or computer generated invitations offer an easy alternative. Encourage the birthday child to add a personal touch to these with a dab or two of glitter glue and a few beads.

TREAT BAGS

These are great as they enable children to take home any party favours that they have accumulated. Instead of setting out all the food on the party table, you may prefer to insert sweets and packets of potato crisps into the bags, to be enjoyed at the children's leisure. They are also ideal for a slice of birthday cake (wrapped in a serviette). A nice gesture is to exchange them for the gift when the birthday child opens his or her presents near the end of the party. Include a card in the treat bag that says: 'Thank you so much for making my day special.' Make the bags in advance and your efforts will be rewarded when you see the delight on the recipients' faces!

DRESSING UP

Most children enjoy fancy dress parties, but if you add this stipulation to the invitation keep the expectations simple to ensure that all the children will be able to participate. Keep a few clothing items and accessories on hand for children who fail to arrive in fancy dress.

PARTY FOOD

The techniques that I have used for the cakes and other treats are very simple and require only basic decorating tools. A toothpick and tweezers are invaluable aids. For icing, the star nozzle is a favourite of mine, as I believe that it provides a neater overall appearance. Sugar paste is readily available at baking supply stores and can easily be coloured using powdered food colourings.

I have used a limited range of ingredients (cupcakes, cones and biscuits for example) and adapted them according to the theme. The cones always lend a special charm to the party table display because of their height.

Plan ahead and make the food in advance. Cakes and biscuits can be baked ahead of time and frozen. It is preferable to bake and freeze the cake before cutting out the various shapes, as the frozen cake will be less crumbly. Coat the cut edges with a thin layer of icing whilst still frozen. The larger cakes are easy to assemble but will require more time. Their visual impact is worth the extra effort and I have heard many a delighted squeal from guests when they have been presented.

Quantities for the recipes in the party food section are not provided, as these will vary according to the number of guests. Colour schemes may be altered.

To enhance the visual impact of the party food, I use simple, inexpensive toys and also take advantage of the huge selection of sweets available. When using sweets on the cakes and other treats remember to consider the age of the children and refrain from using for example, hard sweets for the toddlers' parties. Toys, too, should be age related so that small objects that may be swallowed don't constitute a danger for the little ones.

GAMES AND ACTIVITIES

I have suggested that the winner receives a prize and the rest receive a small token. These may be in the form of stickers or similar inexpensive items. Discount stores and others offer a variety of packs of erasers, etc. that may be split and used to ensure that none of the children feel excluded. The games have been provided as inspiration and to assist with party planning, but you may prefer to hire entertainment. Consult your local directory and remember to book in advance.

When the party is held at an outside venue, check the facilities ahead of time. Ensure that you have sufficient, secure transport. Enlist the help of friends so that children are supervised throughout the event. Accompany all children to the toilets or other facilities. Before departure, divide children into groups and delegate each to a helper so that there is a clear understanding of who is responsible for each child. For younger children, you may colour code the different groups to avoid confusion.

THANK-YOU NOTES

Children should adopt this courtesy from an early age. Choosing a gift requires time and thought and the guest will be delighted to receive a note of thanks. Keep the note short and, if possible, have the birthday child write it personally. Make a list of the gifts and who gave them while the child unwraps them, otherwise it may be difficult to recall who gave what.

Baby's 1st

SETTING THE SCENE

Change the pretty pinks for boyish blues if the birthday star is a boy.
Some of these ideas will also work well for a Stork Party.

* Cut out number ones (see template, page 162) in varying sizes from cardboard, spray pink and decorate with silver stars, glitter, or as preferred. Attach the largest of these to the front gate together with a bunch of pink balloons. Attach the rest of the numbers to the walls of the party area.

* Drape lengths of streamers in shades of pink over the garden shrubs.

* Cover the party table with a pink cloth. Create a canopy above the table by draping pink streamers from the centre of the ceiling to the edges. Twist the streamers before draping to create a softer effect.

* Cut out stars from cardboard (see template, page 162), spray them pink, decorate with glitter and use fishing line to suspend them from the ceiling so that they hang at varying heights above the table. Make a star for each guest and use glitter glue to write his or her name on the star. Present the guests with their particular star 'mobile' to take home at the end of the party.

* Attach bundles of pink balloons to the corners of the room or party area. (The balloons are for decorative purposes only and should not be distributed to the little ones. Dispose of any broken pieces immediately if any balloons should pop.)

* Empty your child's toy box to find suitable toys that may be placed on the table and scattered about the party area, as well as throughout the house. Shop for babies' bath toys, which are available at good prices from discount toy shops and are ideal for table décor and for use in the treat bags.

* Remember to have a supply of paper towels and wipes available for spills and to remedy sticky little hands and faces. Place these in an attractive container that will blend with the décor.

* Mums or child minders will have to be included in the invitation and a table should be set aside for their catering needs. Continue the pink colour scheme for this and decorate the table accordingly.

* The duration of this party should be no longer than 1½–2 hours.

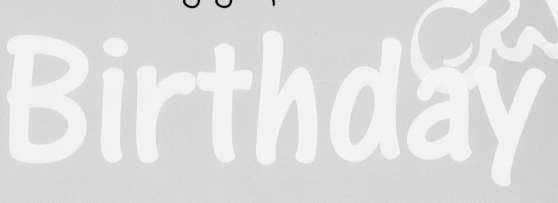

Recommended age group: 1–2

Birthday

INVITATIONS

YOU WILL NEED:
Pink notepaper
Pen
Pink curling ribbon
Dolls' feeding bottles
Pink board paper nametags
Paper punch

1. Write the invitation details (see Suggested Wording) on the notepaper. Roll it up, tie with curling ribbon and place inside the bottle.
2. Write the guest's name on the nametag, punch a hole in the centre of one side edge and attach the tag to the neck of the bottle with curling ribbon.

SUGGESTED WORDING
(Child's name), a very special baby, is turning one!
Toddle over to: (address) on (date)
Playtime starts at: (time party starts)
Playtime ends at: (time party ends)
RSVP: Number One's Mum at (phone number) by (date)

TREAT BAGS

YOU WILL NEED:
Pink board paper nametags
Pen
Paper punch
Pink gift bags
Pink curling ribbon
Pink plastic dummies (pacifiers)

1. Write the guest's name on the nametag, punch a hole in the centre of one side edge and attach the tag to the handle of the bag with curling ribbon.
2. Thread a length of curling ribbon through the loop of the dummy (pacifier) and attach it to the handle so that it hangs against the outside of the bag.

GAMES AND ACTIVITIES

Free play is advised for children of this age. Set up various play stations using any toys that your child may have. You may need to borrow from friends to increase the options. A few suggestions that are sure to amuse the little ones are: a ball pond; riding toys such as tricycles and push bikes; building blocks; pulling toys such as wagons that may be piled high with toys; pushing toys such as dolls' prams; activity toys that have dials, knobs and push buttons; musical toys.

Empty cardboard boxes with lids and bottoms removed make wonderful adventure tunnels for little explorers. You may paint these with pink craft paint and decorate with crepe ribbons to add to the appeal.

BATHTIME BUBBLES CAKE

1 x Basic Cake (page 160) – 300 x 240 mm
500 g sugar paste
Powdered food colouring – gold, yellow, pink, blue
1–2 drops white alcohol or water
Icing (page 160) – pink, pale blue, white
1 x small doll
White edible glitter
1 x small toy duck

1. Bake the cake according to the recipe and leave to cool completely.
2. Fashion a tap from a small piece of sugar paste and set aside to firm. (I used a small star cutter for the top of the tap, but you may shape your own as preferred.)
3. Dilute a pinch of gold powdered food colouring in the alcohol and coat the tap. Set aside.
4. Cut the cake in half across the width.
5. Cut out an oval bath shape – measuring about 170 mm in length x 110 mm wide – from one of the cakes. Reserve the cutout section.
6. Coat the other cake lightly with a layer of icing and place the cake with the cutout on top of this. Coat the whole cake, including the inner section of the bath trough, with a layer of pink icing.
7. Remove the legs from the doll and insert the torso into the trough.
8. Cut the reserved piece of cake in half horizontally and place back in the trough, cut to fit, and wedge against the doll for support.
9. Use about two fistfuls of sugar paste and colour one yellow and the other pink. Roll out on a flat surface to 3–4 mm thick and cut into 15 mm squares for the tiles.
10. Starting from the centre of one outer side edge of the cake, lay the tiles in rows as illustrated, working inwards to the edge of the bath trough and cutting the tiles to fit where necessary.
11. Complete the sides of the cake by coating with pink icing. Use the star nozzle for a softer effect.
12. Cover the surface of the cake inside the bath trough with pale blue icing, roughening it with the tip of a knife. Add small threads of white icing and pull through with a toothpick to complete the water-like effect.
13. Add a dab of blue icing to the doll's head, hand and upper torso and attach small balls of sugar paste to resemble bubbles. Place bubbles randomly on the surface of the water and dust the bubbles and water surface with edible glitter.
14. Place the duck in position on the water and use a small dab of icing to secure the tap to the side edge of the bath.

PARTY FOOD

Golden Geese

Party Cupcakes (page 161)
Gold foil cookie cups (baking cases)
Icing (page 160) – pale pink
Pink edible glitter
Yellow-and-pink marshmallow ducks

1. Bake the cupcakes in the cookie cups according to the recipe and leave to cool.
2. Use the star nozzle to ice the cupcakes.
3. Sprinkle with edible glitter and perch a marshmallow duck on top.

Rattling Stars

Note: Watch the little ones with the rattles! Remove them when serving and give them to the mums to keep as a memento.

Easy biscuits (page 161)
Star cookie cutter or template (page 162)
Drinking straw
Icing (page 160) – pink
Pink edible glitter
Small pink balls
Pink ribbon
Pink toy plastic rattles

1. Prepare the biscuit dough as per the recipe.
2. Use the cookie cutter or template to cut out star shapes. Use the drinking straw to make a hole near the edge of one of the pointed tips.
3. Bake according to instructions and leave to cool.
4. Coat the biscuits with icing and sprinkle with edible glitter.
5. Attach a pink ball to each point of the star.
6. Tie a length of ribbon around the handle of the rattle and thread through the hole in the biscuit before knotting the ends together to form a loop.

Wacky Waddle Surprises

Ingredients listed are for one treat.

1 x Marie biscuit or Rich Tea™ biscuit
Icing (page 160) – yellow, pink
Yellow vermicelli
Sugar paste – coloured pale pink with powdered food colouring
2 x wafer cookie cups
Small, soft sweets that are suitable for a one year old
1 x white mini marshmallow
2 x small pink balls

1. Coat the Marie biscuit with yellow icing and sprinkle lightly with vermicelli.
2. Knead the sugar paste until soft. Work in the food colouring until a pastel shade is obtained.
3. Mould two duck feet and position them on the front half of the biscuit.
4. Place one cookie cup on the Marie biscuit base and fill with sweets.
5. Coat the rim of the cookie cup with a thin layer of icing and place the upended second cup on top of this, pressing down lightly to seal.
6. Mould a flat piece of sugar paste to resemble an open beak. Set aside until firm. Use a blob of icing to attach the beak to the front of the cookie cups.
7. Cut two thin slices off each end of the marshmallow and attach with icing for the eyes.
8. Dip one side of the pink balls in icing and attach to the marshmallows.
9. To finish off, use the star nozzle to pull out a tuft of 'feathers' on the top of the upper cookie cup.

Quacking Treats

Pink ice cream
Small clear plastic containers
1 x toy yellow duck per serving

1. Place a scoop of pink ice cream in the container.
2. Top with the toy duck, which the guests will be delighted to take home.

SETTING THE SCENE

Girls enjoy pirate parties just as much as boys so they should definitely not be excluded from this one! Stipulate that no 'weapons' that could cause harm to any of the children should be brought to the party.

* This party is best held outdoors, but provision should always be made in case of bad weather. Fly a Jolly Roger (black flag with white skull and crossbones) from the front gate so that all pirates can easily identify the venue. (Use the template on page 162.)

* Place a 'gangplank' in the entrance for guests to 'board the ship'. Create a treasure chest in which guests may place their presents as they enter the party area. Spray a large cardboard box with gold paint and decorate with toy necklaces and fake jewels. Sprinkle sea sand around the base and add a few gold-covered chocolate coins as well as seashells and other treasures to enhance the effect.

* Lay blue crepe paper over the party table and cover with blue organza fabric that has been scrunched up in parts to resemble a wavy ocean. Place toy fish and other sea creatures on the table.

* Decorate the party area with blue balloons. Create a desert island by using potted palms placed on a bed of sea sand. A plastic toy skeleton outstretched on the sand will thrill the young pirates.

* Make a Jolly Roger to hang on the wall behind the party table. Enlarge the template on page 162, as required, and use white fabric paint to transfer to black cotton fabric. If preferred trace the template onto white felt fabric. Cut out and use fabric glue to attach to the rectangular black material.

* Use the same template to make small Jolly Roger flags that may be attached to wooden skewers and inserted into the various dishes on the table.

* Set up a tattoo booth so that the pirates may be 'inked' while waiting for the rest of the 'crew' to arrive. You may also include face paints to add a moustache and/or a scar. Remember to have a few dress-up items available in the event that a guest arrives without fancy dress.

Recommended age group: 6-10

Plundering Pirates

INVITATIONS

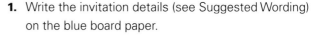

YOU WILL NEED:
Blue board paper
Pen
Paper punch
Toy black eye patches
Light and dark blue
curling ribbon

1. Write the invitation details (see Suggested Wording) on the blue board paper.
2. Punch a hole in the centre along one side edge.
3. Thread the eye patch elastic through the hole of the card and knot to secure. (Guests may wear these to the party!)
4. Enhance with curling ribbon.

SUGGESTED WORDING

Ahoy (guest's name)!
Captain (birthday child's name) is having a Pirate Party on (date).
Please board the ship at pier: (party address)
The anchor will be hoisted at: (time party starts)
Ship returns to port at: (time party ends)
Dress: Like a pirate!
RSVP: First Mate at (phone number) by (date)

TREAT BAGS

YOU WILL NEED:
Jolly Rodger template (page 162)
Blue gift bags
Scissors
Craft glue
Beads
Blue paper board nametags
Pen
Paper punch
Light and dark blue curling ribbon

1. Enlarge the template to fit the bag, then cut it out and glue to the front.
2. Glue a pile of 'jewels' (beads) to the bag.
3. Write the guest's name on the blue nametag, punch a hole near the edge and attach the card to the handle of the bag with curling ribbon.

GAMES AND ACTIVITIES

Message in a Bottle

YOU WILL NEED:

Paper notelets with forfeits*, one per guest

Pencil

Curling ribbon or elastic bands

Small, clear plastic bottles with lids, one per guest

1 x tub of water

1 x basket or similar container containing small
   tokens, one per guest plus one or two extra

Roll each notelet around the pencil, and secure with a small piece of curling ribbon or an elastic band. Remove the pencil and insert the message into the bottle. Seal the bottle and place it in the tub of water.

The children take turns to retrieve a bottle and then act out their task in front of the others. On completion, the child may select a token from the basket.

* Examples: 'Hop on your peg leg (one leg) for one minute'; 'The captain's parrot has flown away – use parrot squawks (x 10) to call it back'; 'Find five buried coins in a bucket of sand'; 'The ship has sprung a leak – sit in the water that has swamped the deck'; 'Cross the swamp without waking the crocodiles (walk across a strip of bubble wrap without making popping noises)'.

Treasure Hunt

YOU WILL NEED (PER TEAM):

1 x set of pirate features (see template, page 162)

1 x set of clues (according to possible hiding places)

1 x paper plate

1 x glue stick

Hide the pirate features ahead of time, with different hiding places for each team. Divide the children into two or more teams. On starter's orders, each team must use their set of clues to search for the features.

As each feature is found, it must be glued to the underside of the plate before the team can move on to the next location.

The winning team is the one that completes their pirate in the shortest time. Each child on the winning team receives a prize, the rest receive a token.

Walk the Plank

For younger children, use parallel strips of masking tape placed on the ground instead of using the plank.

YOU WILL NEED:

1 x plank – 2 m long x 15 cm wide x 5 cm thick

2 x bricks for support

1 x blindfold

Place the plank on the bricks and have each child walk across in turn. If a child fails to negotiate the plank successfully, he or she is eliminated.

The task should become more difficult with each round and you should add a new obstacle, according to the ability of the children, for example: a blindfold (assist children to get onto the plank), instruct them to walk backwards or hop on one leg, have two pirates start simultaneously at opposite ends and pass each other in the centre of the plank, without toppling off. The game continues in this manner until you have a single winner who receives a prize. The rest of the children receive a token. You may elect to have more than one winner if the children are particularly agile!

Load the Cannons

YOU WILL NEED (PER TEAM):

10 or more (allow for breakages) water-filled balloons

2 x cardboard boxes or similar containers

Divide the children into two teams that should line up alongside each other with one metre's gap between each child in the row. Place the water balloons in the containers at one end of the team, with empty containers at the opposite end. On starter's orders, the child on each team nearest the 'cannonballs' must pick one up and toss it to the next child in the row, who in turn passes it down the line to the last child, who must place the 'cannonball' in the empty container.

The game continues with the 'cannonballs' being fed down the line as fast as possible. The winners are the team with the most 'cannonballs' in their container in the shortest time. The winning team receives a prize, the rest receive a token.

PARTY FOOD

Skull Cakes

Party Cupcakes (page 161)
Gold foil cookie cups (baking cases)
Icing (page 160) – blue
Skull and crossbones cocktail sticks
White bone-shaped sweets

1. Prepare the cupcakes according to the recipe, bake in the foil cookie cups and leave to cool completely.
2. Coat the top of the cupcakes with icing, insert the cocktail sticks and decorate with bone sweets.

Desert Island Ice Cream

Have all the accessories and decorative pieces prepared in advance and assemble just before serving.

Liquorice layers from Liquorice Allsorts™
Round chocolate-coated biscuits
Icing (page 160) – green
Plastic parfait dishes or sugared wafer cups
Palm tree drink cooler*
Blue ice cream (soften white ice cream slightly, add blue powdered food colouring and return to the freezer to harden)
Plastic toy skeletons
Prestik® or Blu-tac™, if required

1. Cut the liquorice layers into sharks' fins, allowing two to three per serving.
2. Use the star nozzle to cover the top of the biscuit with green icing. (You must prepare these in advance.)
3. Place a palm tree in the parfait dish or wafer cup and add the ice cream.
4. Place the prepared biscuit on top of the ice cream and add the fins to the 'water'.
5. Rest the skeleton against the tree, securing with a small dab of Prestik® if necessary.

* This is a swizzle stick that is filled with liquid so that it can be frozen to keep drinks cool.

Booming Biscuits

Remove the toothpicks before eating!

Wafer biscuits
Icing (page 160) – blue
Liquorice cables
Toothpicks with cellophane frills
Flat round sweets
Small ball sweets

1. Cover the top of the wafer biscuit with icing.
2. For the base of the cannon, cut a 15 mm piece of liquorice and place it across the width of the biscuit.
3. Push the toothpick into one end of a second piece of liquorice, 80 mm long, to form the barrel, and rest it on the liquorice base. The bottom end of the barrel should rest on the biscuit.
4. Place a flat round sweet on either side of the base for wheels. Arrange 'cannonballs' around the cannon.

Perilous Point Lighthouse

Flat-bottomed wafer ice-cream cones (or use the tapered variety and snip off the end)
Sweets of choice
Marie biscuits or Rich Tea™ biscuits
Icing (page 160) – blue, red, white
Sour lemon ball
Liquorice Allsorts™ for door, or as preferred
Silver balls

1. Fill the wafer cone with sweets of choice.
2. Coat a Marie biscuit with blue icing and place it over the open end of the cone. Upend so that the biscuit forms the base. Use the star nozzle to pipe rows of stars around the entire cone. Start with two rows of blue stars around the base and continue with red and white stripes, piping two rows of each colour until the cone is covered.
3. Coat the top of the cone with white icing and place the lemon ball in position.
4. Cut a door from a layer of the Liquorice Allsorts™. Place on the first row of red stars. Add a silver ball for the doorknob.

PLUNDERING PIRATE CAKE

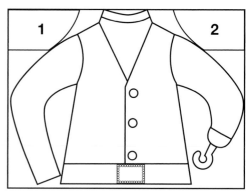

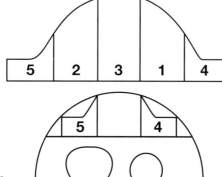

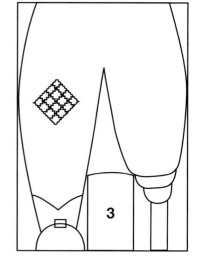

2½ x Basic Cake (page 160) –

    two x 300 mm x 240 mm rectangular cakes;

    one x 200 mm round cake

Icing (page 160) – flesh-coloured, black, brown, red, white,

    blue, yellow

Small ball of white sugar paste

4 x white bone-shaped sweets

1 x liquorice strap

Small gold balls

4 x large gold balls

12 x Liquorice Allsorts Mini™

3 x Smarties®

Multi-coloured candy cane

1 x large googly eye

1 x plastic toy eye patch

1 x thin strip of liquorice

1 x imitation gold earring

1 x decorative silver foil anchor

1.   Bake the cakes as directed and leave to cool completely.

2.   Cut out and assemble the cakes as shown above. For the hat section: Cut section 3 from between the legs, then flank it with sections 1 and 2, which are cut from alongside the bodice. Cut sections 4 and 5 from the head (round cake) and join to sections 1 and 2. Ensure that the surfaces are level. Use off-cuts to assist with 'padding'.

3.   Ice the cake as follows: flesh-coloured icing for the face, black stars for the hat and boot, brown stars for the peg leg and the arm stump and red-and-white stripes for the shirt. The waistcoat is iced in red with a border of stars around the edge as well as down the centre front, and the trousers are blue. Use the tip of a knife to roughen the surface of the icing on the waistcoat and trousers.

4.   Roll out the sugar paste to 2–4 mm thick and cut into a skull shape. Attach to the hat and position the bone-shaped sweets so that it resembles a skull and crossbones. Cut the liquorice strap to fit the waist and add a buckle made from the small gold balls, attaching each with a small dab of icing. Place the four large gold balls in position on the boot. Assemble the patch on the trousers using the Liquorice Allsorts Mini™ sweets and place the buttons (Smarties®) down the centre of the waistcoat. Gently insert the candy cane into the arm stump so that the hook protrudes.

5.   Use the mouth from the facial features' template (page 162) as a guide and fill in with piped red stars. Add a black tooth cut from the liquorice layer of a Liquorice Allsorts Mini™ sweet. Add the googly eye and the eye patch. Cut a thin strip of liquorice for the eyebrow. Add the wedge-shaped nose, which is cut from a layer of a Liquorice Allsorts Mini™. Use the star nozzle and a pull-out motion to add the (sun bleached!) yellow hair.

6.   Tie 4 or 5 toothpicks together in a bundle with an elastic band or adhesive tape. Dip in black food colouring and use to create beard stubble on the chin and cheeks. (If using powdered colouring, dilute in a drop of water or white alcohol.) Finally add the earring and place the anchor on the waistcoat to complete this delightful chap.

Hearty

SETTING THE SCENE

This theme also works well for a Valentine's Day party and is an easy fancy dress option. Although the colours used here are red and white, you may change the colour scheme according to preference.

* Start preparing for this party well in advance because the more hearts you can make, the better the impact. Enlist the help of the entire family and enjoy many happy moments around the craft table!

* Cut out as many cardboard hearts as you can manage (to fill the party area) and colour with craft paint or spray. Restrict the colours to red and white.

* Attach a large red heart to the front gate and add a bunch of red and white balloons tied together with red curling ribbon. Lay out a path of hearts from the gate to the party venue.

* Create a string curtain of hearts at the front door. Make red and white cardboard hearts and decorate with glitter. Punch a hole near the top centre edge and string a few on a length of fishing line, knotting well to secure. Make as many strings as you will need and suspend them from the doorframe.

* Set up a face-painting booth near the front entrance so that guests may be adorned with a heart as they arrive. Enlist the help of a friend to handle this task.

* Attach sheets of red cellophane to the windows in the party area.

* Create a canopy above the party table by draping strips of twisted red and white streamers from the centre of the ceiling to the outer edges.

* Suspend cardboard hearts from the ceiling using fishing line (guests may take these home at the end of the party). Tie red and white balloons in the corners of the room and add heart-shaped balloons for extra impact. Attach huge cardboard hearts to the walls and decorate them with glitter and ribbon.

* Cover the table with a red cloth or red crepe paper and top with a contrasting white overlay. Sprinkle the table with heart confetti. Use heart-shaped plates and dishes where possible and make serving platters from firm cardboard painted red and/or white with non-toxic craft spray.

Recommended age group: 6–12

Party

INVITATIONS

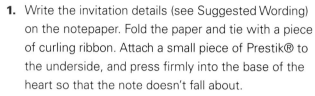

YOU WILL NEED (PER INVITATION):

Red felt-tip marker
White notepaper
Red and white curling ribbon
Prestik® or Blu-tac™
Clear plastic heart-shaped container
Heart confetti
White board paper nametag
Red glitter pen
Paper punch

1. Write the invitation details (see Suggested Wording) on the notepaper. Fold the paper and tie with a piece of curling ribbon. Attach a small piece of Prestik® to the underside, and press firmly into the base of the heart so that the note doesn't fall about.
2. Add a pinch or two of heart confetti, then close the container.
3. Write the guest's name on the board paper with the glitter pen and attach a confetti heart.
4. Punch a hole in one corner of the nametag and attach it to the loop of the container using the curling ribbon.

SUGGESTED WORDING

Skip to the beat at (child's name)'s party on (date).
The pulsating venue: (address)
The beat starts at: (time party starts)
The beat ends at: (time party ends)
RSVP: Queen of Hearts at (phone number) by (date)
Dress: Red or white with lots of hearts!

TREAT BAGS

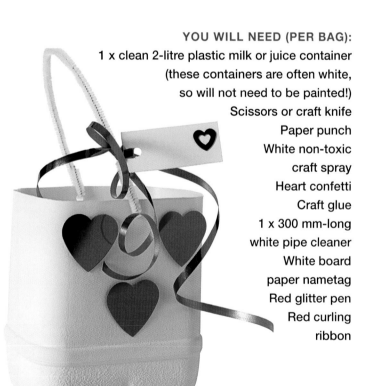

YOU WILL NEED (PER BAG):

1 x clean 2-litre plastic milk or juice container (these containers are often white, so will not need to be painted!)
Scissors or craft knife
Paper punch
White non-toxic craft spray
Heart confetti
Craft glue
1 x 300 mm-long white pipe cleaner
White board paper nametag
Red glitter pen
Red curling ribbon

1. Cut the top section from the container, just below the handle, and discard.
2. Use the paper punch to make a hole on either side, near the rim of the container.
3. If necessary, spray the container with white craft spray and leave to dry.
4. Attach the large confetti hearts to the container with craft glue.
5. Thread the ends of the pipe cleaner through the holes in the container and bend the ends to secure the handle.
6. Punch a hole near one corner of the nametag and write the guest's name with the glitter pen. Glue on a small confetti heart and tie the tag to the handle with curling ribbon.

GAMES AND ACTIVITIES

Rhythmic Hearts

YOU WILL NEED:

Cardboard hearts, one less than the number of guests
Music

Place the hearts on a table in the centre of the play area. Start the music and instruct the children to dance about the table in a wide circle, moving in time to the music. When the music stops, each child must grab a heart from the table. The child who is left without a heart is out.

The hearts are then placed back on the table, with one being removed at the end of each round. The game continues in the same manner until there is a winner. The winner receives a prize, the rest receive tokens.

Mend the Broken Heart

YOU WILL NEED:

Cardboard hearts cut in half down the centre, sufficient so that each child has a half of a heart
Container of small prizes (one for each guest)
Written instructions on the back of each half of a heart (duplicate each instruction so that it appears twice, enabling each child to find a partner)*

Have each child choose half a heart. Instruct them to carry out the instructions written on the back of the heart. While they do this they must try to find their partners, who will, of course, be acting out the same instruction. When the children have found their partners they must line up, one pair behind the other, at a demarcated finishing line, until all have partners. Each pair must act out their 'forfeit' for all to view, before choosing a prize from the container.

* The instructions may be: 'Hop on one leg'; 'Bark like a dog'; 'Skip backwards'; 'Moo like a cow'; 'Cry like a baby'; and so on. For older children, you may increase the degree of difficulty as preferred. If there are an uneven number of children, write something like 'You are very special – sit behind the finishing line immediately'. This child may have the opportunity to choose a prize first.

Throbbing Steps!

YOU WILL NEED:

List of predetermined targets, known only to the game co-ordinator
Music

Predetermined targets in the party area are listed on a piece of paper that is kept by the co-ordinator.

Start the music and instruct the children to dance about the room. When the music stops, the children must freeze on the spot.

The game co-ordinator then reveals the first target on the list and the child standing closest to it is out. (For a large group, you may decide to eliminate more than one child with each round.) The game continues in this manner until one child remains. The winner receives a prize, the rest receive tokens.

Heart-to-Heart Race

YOU WILL NEED (PER TEAM):

Cardboard box, basket or similar container
Cardboard hearts (as per the number of guests on each team)
Blindfold

Divide the children into two or more teams. Place the containers with the cardboard hearts at a predetermined distance from each team.

Have the children line up one behind the other and blindfold the first child in each row.

On starter's orders, the blindfolded child is spun around three times and has to fetch a heart from the container. The rest of the team must guide the child by shouting directions, such as 'move to the left', 'walk straight ahead', and so on.

When the child has picked up a heart, she must remove her blindfold and race back to her team.

The blindfold is handed to the next child and the game continues in the same manner until a team has all its hearts. The winning team receives a prize, the rest receive tokens.

PARTY FOOD

Such a Sweetheart!

Red drinking straws
Prestik® or Blu-tac™
Small plastic containers
Heart-shaped sweets
Circles of red tulle (the diameter will depend on the
    size of the container used)
Red curling ribbon and/or white curling ribbon with
    red hearts
Red board paper hearts
Silver glitter pen

1. Attach one end of the straw with Prestik® to
   the centre of the container and fill the container
   with sweets.
2. Place the container in the centre of the tulle circle.
   Gather up the tulle around the straw and tie with
   curling ribbon.
3. Write the guest's name on the paper heart with
   the glitter pen and attach it to the straw with a
   blob of Prestik®.

The Heart of the Matter

Party Cupcakes (page 161)
Red food colouring
Silver cookie cups (baking cases)
Icing (page 160) – white
Red edible glitter
Red curling ribbon
Red heart-shaped lollipop, or heart-shaped sweets
    attached to a toothpick
Silver balls

1. Prepare the cupcake batter according to the recipe.
2. Colour the cupcake mixture with the red food
   colouring, and bake in the cookie cups as per the
   recipe. Leave to cool completely.
3. Coat the top of the cupcake with white icing and
   sprinkle with edible glitter.
4. Tie curling ribbon around the stick of the lollipop and
   insert it into the centre of the cupcake.
5. Decorate with silver balls as illustrated.

Message from the Heart

Sugar paste – white
Small heart-shaped cookie cutter
Easy Biscuits (page 161)
Heart-shaped cookie cutter or template (page 163)
Drinking straw
Icing (page 160) – red
Red board paper
Scissors
Paper punch
Red or white ribbons with red hearts – 160 mm lengths

1. Roll out the sugar paste to 2–4 mm thick and cut out
   hearts with the small cutter. Set aside.
2. Prepare the biscuit dough as per the recipe. Use the
   larger cookie cutter or template to cut out heart-
   shaped biscuits. Make a hole with the straw near
   one side edge before baking as directed.
3. Leave to cool completely before coating with red
   icing (use the straw to keep the hole open).
4. Place a sugar paste heart in the centre of the biscuit.
5. Cut out hearts from the board paper, then write a
   message on each, for example: 'You make a heart
   skip a beat.' Punch a hole in the paper and attach one
   end of the ribbon. Thread the other end through the
   hole in the biscuit and knot to secure.

Tender Hearts

Meringues (page 161) – recipe makes about 20 hearts
Heart template (page 163)
Sugar paste – red
Small heart-shaped cookie cutter
Icing (page 160) – white

1. Prepare the meringue according to the recipe.
2. Use the template to outline hearts on greaseproof
   paper. Line a baking tray with the marked paper and
   use a star nozzle to pipe heart shapes to fill the
   traced heart outlines. Smooth the meringue with the
   back of a teaspoon, and then bake as directed.
3. Roll out the sugar paste to 2–4 mm thick and cut out
   hearts. Attach to the cooled meringues with icing.

HEART-STOPPING CAKE!

1 x Basic Cake (page 160) – one x 200 mm round cake; one x 200 mm square cake
Icing (page 160) – red
1 kg sugar paste (this will allow extra for the small hearts for the party treats on page 24)
Red powdered food colouring
Silver balls
Ribbon – 120 cm long x 35 mm wide (optional)

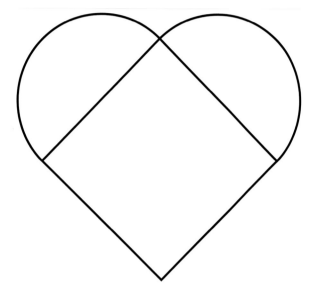

1. Bake the cakes as per the recipe and leave to cool completely.
2. Cut the round cake into two semi-circles and position the cakes as shown above to form a heart shape. Join the sections with icing.
3. Ensure that the tops of the cakes are level – use a serrated knife to trim if necessary.
4. Coat the cake with a thin layer of icing to provide a smooth base for the sugar paste.
5. Colour three-quarters (750 g) of the sugar paste red and roll it out to 3–4 mm thick on a surface that has been dusted with icing sugar. Ensure that you have sufficient to cover the top and sides of the cake.
6. Carefully lay the sugar paste on top of the cake and smooth gently, following the contour of the heart. Trim away the excess from the base of the cake.
7. Use the above cutting guide to create templates for each of the sugar paste hearts that are used to decorate the cake. Make squares and rounds with the following dimensions:
   160 mm – white heart
   120 mm – red heart
   80 mm – white heart
   40 mm – red heart
8. Roll out the sugar paste to 3–4 mm thick and use the templates to cut out the hearts, from the largest to the smallest, and place in descending order on top of the cake.
9. Leave the sugar paste to harden before edging each heart with icing piped through the star nozzle.
10. Enhance the edging with evenly spaced silver balls.
11. Wind the ribbon (if using) around the cake and overlap the edges. Secure with a toothpick. Use small dabs of icing to fix the ribbon to the edge as necessary.

Teddy's

SETTING THE SCENE

The young guests will have to allow their mums to tag along to this beary special party; after all, they will need baby-sitters for their teddies!

* Place a teddy bear wearing a party hat at the entrance. The bear should be 'holding' a board stating the birthday child's name and (relevant age) birthday party. Position paw prints (see template, page 162) leading from the front entrance to the party table. Hang green streamers and/or strips of creeper in the doorway for guests to pass through on their way to Teddy Bear Land.

* Position extra teddy bears in groups on small picnic blankets on the floor of the party area. A doll's plastic tea set will add to the picnic effect. Place potted plants in the party area to add to the woodland effect. Plastic toadstools and small woodland creatures (a squirrel or a mouse) peeping out from behind the plants will enhance the scene. You can also place small pots of flowers or seedlings in strategic positions, but make sure that they are placed where guests won't trip over them.

* Cover the party table with green crepe paper and use a green gingham cloth as an overlay. Create a canopy above the table using 50 mm-wide strips of green crepe paper. Twist the strips before draping them from the centre of the ceiling to the edges. Tie bundles of green balloons in the corners. Use fishing line to suspend teddy bear cutouts (see template, page 162) from the ceiling. These may be distributed to guests at the end of the party. Again using the template on page 162, make strips of teddy bears using craft paper, and attach them to the walls of the party room.

* Mums and child minders will need to be included in the invitation. Set aside a table for their catering needs and continue the theme by covering the table with green crepe paper and a gingham overlay.

* The duration of this party should be no longer than 1½–2 hours.

Recommended age group: 2-4

Picnic

INVITATIONS

YOU WILL NEED:

A2-size sheets of brown board paper
(each sheet makes two invitations if
you use the dimensions provided)
Scissors
Ruler
Pencil
Teddy bear template (page 162)
Black and red felt-tip markers
2 x googly eyes per invitation
1 x coloured bow per invitation
Craft glue
Light brown notepaper
Green glitter pen

1. Cut off a 160 mm-wide x 594 mm-long strip of brown board paper. Mark off four 125 mm sections with a pencil. Cut off and discard the last bit.
2. Fold the paper in concertina fashion along the pencil lines. Place the template on top and trace around it.
3. Cut out the teddy shape along its edges, but don't cut off the ends of the arms. Unfold the chain (you should have four double-sided bears) and decorate the top (front) bear as illustrated below.
4. Cut seven circles from the light brown paper to fit the tummy of each remaining bear. Write one section of details on each bear (see Suggested Wording).
5. Use the glitter pen to write the guest's name across the tummy of the front bear.

SUGGESTED WORDING

1st bear: Guest's name
2nd bear: Celebrate a beary special event on (date)!
3rd bear: (Birthday child's name) is turning (age)
4th bear: Hurry to the woods at (address)
5th bear: The teddy bears gather at (time party starts)
6th bear: Picnic ends at (time party ends)
7th bear: Please bring your teddy bear. (Confirm that your mum is available to mind your teddy while you party!)
8th bear: RSVP: Mummy Bear at (phone number) by (date)

TREAT BAGS

YOU WILL NEED (PER BAG):
1 x clean 2-litre ice-cream tub
Craft knife or scissors
1 x 300 mm-long green pipe cleaner for handle
Masking tape
Pinking shears

1 x 350 mm square of green gingham cloth (or use a paper gingham serviette)
Green glitter pen
Green curling ribbon

1. Punch a small hole near each side edge of the ice-cream tub lid using a craft knife or scissors. Insert the pipe cleaner to form a handle, bending each end against the underside of the lid. Secure with tape.
2. Use the pinking shears to neaten the edges of the gingham square. Line the tub with the cloth, allowing the outer edges to protrude from the tub when sealed with the lid.
3. Write the guest's name on the lid of the 'picnic basket' with the glitter pen. Attach a length of curling ribbon to the handle of the basket.

GAMES AND ACTIVITIES

Children of this age are generally too young to play the usual party games and don't always understand the allocation of prizes. Set up play stations where they can amuse themselves. Suggestions for the play stations:

A sand pit with various toys, spades and buckets (outdoor activity); prams and wagons for giving teddies a ride; dolls' clothes for dressing Teddy; a ball pond; modelling dough table; bubble fun (with assistance from the mums and child minders – outdoor activity); tattoo booth (manned by an obliging friend! Mums can also join in the spirit of the party by choosing a stick-on tattoo for themselves. Little ones will be delighted to see their mums adorned in this manner.)

If you do want a game for the guests, all tiny tots enjoy playing 'Ring a Ring o' Roses'. Mums and teddies will be able to join in with this one too.

For those mums who don't remember the format of this activity, the children form a circle and join hands, and then walk round while singing:

Ring a Ring o' Roses
A pocketful of posies
Ashes! Ashes!
We all fall down

Everyone then falls down amidst much laughter! Repeat the activity once or twice.

PARTY FOOD

Trinket to Treasure

These treats are ideal take-home gifts for guests – attach a small card to the handle as a thank-you note.

Wafer cookie cups
Pipe cleaners, about 180 mm long
Marie biscuits or Rich Tea™ biscuits
Icing (page 160) – green
Gold balls
Small toy teddies
Small sweets of choice

1. Use a toothpick to make a small hole in opposite sides of the cookie cup, near the upper edge.
2. Gently feed each end of the pipe cleaner through the hole, working from the inside of the cookie cup, to make a handle for the basket. Turn up the ends.
3. Coat the Marie biscuit with icing. Place the basket in the centre, pressing down gently. Pipe stars around the edge of the biscuit and attach a gold ball to each.
4. Place a teddy and sweets in the basket.

Picnic in the Shade

Party Cupcakes (page 161)
Gold foil cookie cups (baking cases)
Icing (page 160) – green
Sugar paste – yellow
Sugared jelly teddies
Pink balls
Mini sugared jelly sweets
Paper parasols (remove before little ones start to eat)

1. Bake the cupcakes in the gold foil cookie cups as per the recipe and leave to cool completely. Coat the cupcake with a layer of green icing.
2. Roll out the sugar paste to 2–4 mm thick. Cut out a square (40 mm), and use a sharp knife to create a fringe around the edges. Place the 'blanket' over the cupcake, leaving some of the green 'grass' exposed.
3. Use icing to attach two teddies to the blanket and a pink ball to the top of a sugared jelly sweet. Place on the blanket. Place the parasol behind the teddies.

Trendy Teddy

Easy Biscuits (page 161)
Teddy bear cookie cutters
White chocolate discs
Icing (page 160) – chocolate
Chocolate chips
Gold balls
Red powdered food colouring diluted in a few drops of white alcohol or water
Fine craft brush or non-toxic food decorating pen
Liquorice Allsorts™
Mini Smarties®

1. Prepare the biscuit dough as per the recipe. Cut out the biscuits and bake as directed. Leave to cool.
2. Coat the back of a white chocolate disc with icing and attach for the face. Place two chocolate chips for the eyes and attach a gold ball to each with icing. Cut another chocolate chip in half for the nose. Use the brush and colouring to paint on a mouth.
3. Use the star nozzle to cover the rest of the teddy with chocolate icing. Cut a bow tie from a Liquorice Allsorts™ layer. Add the mini Smarties® as buttons.

Beary Sweet Friend

Wafer biscuits
Icing (page 160) – white
Mini marshmallows
Mallow Bake™ marshmallows
Hundreds and thousands
Silver balls
Chocolate chips
Liquorice Allsorts Mini™

1. Coat the wafer biscuit with a layer of icing.
2. Place 2 x mini marshmallows for the body and head, 8 x Mallow Bake™ marshmallows for the legs, arms and ears. Sprinkle hundreds and thousands around the teddy. Attach silver balls for the eyes. Cut a chocolate chip in half and use one half for the mouth.
3. Cut a bowtie from a coloured layer of a Liquorice Allsorts Mini™ and attach to the neck.

Fun at the Park Cake

3 x wafer ice-cream cones
2 x Basic Cake (page 160) – two x 300 x 240 mm
Icing (page 160) – green
Caramel crunch
1 x small toy seesaw (or use an upturned wafer cookie cup and a long, straight lollipop – stick removed – and support the teddies with a blob of icing)
Chocolate stones or chocolate chips
Sour cherry flower-shaped sweets
Toothpicks
Candy necklace flower-shaped sweets
Small gold balls

Gingham fabric, approximately 80 mm square, edges neatened with pinking shears
1 x small toy basket or similar container
Mini Astros™
1 x round sugared jelly sweet for the picnic 'cake'
5 x chocolate jewels for paving stones
6 x small toy teddy bears
1 x small blob of Prestik® or Blu-Tac™
2 x lengths of florist's wire, about 180 mm and 140 mm
2 x small toy white doves
4 x small toy or iced butterflies
1 x small paper parasol

1. Make the 'trees' the night before you make the rest of the cake so that they have time to set. This will make them easier to handle. Upend the ice-cream cones and, using the star nozzle, pull out the icing to create the branches on the trees. Work in a circular pattern from the base to the top. (I place the cones on a small plate, which allows me to turn them around with ease. I set the trees aside overnight and use a spatula to lift them the next morning.)

2. Bake the cakes as per the recipe and leave to cool completely.

3. Place the cakes on the cake board parallel to each other with the longer sides joined together with icing. Coat the rest of the cake with a thin layer of green icing.

4. Use a toothpick to mark out the forest area and the play area before piping on the grass with the star nozzle.

5. Place the trees in the forest area and sprinkle the caramel crunch to cover the remaining surface of the forest.

6. Position the seesaw in the play area and scatter the chocolate stones over the surface of that section.

7. Place the sour cherry flower sweets in position, using a toothpick to support each one. (Remember to remove the toothpicks before the little ones eat.)

8. Arrange the candy necklace flower sweets as illustrated, attaching a small gold ball in the centre of each with a dab of icing.

9. Place the picnic cloth and basket filled with Mini Astros™ in position. Attach gold balls to the round sugared jelly sweet to make a 'cake', and place on the picnic cloth.

10. Lay a pathway of chocolate jewel paving stones from the play area to the picnic spot.

11. Position the teddy bears as illustrated.

12. Attach a small blob of Prestik® to one end of each of the lengths of florist's wire and place a dove on top. Insert the wire into the cake as illustrated so that the doves hover above the trees.

13. Attach the butterflies to the flower-shaped jelly sweets using a dab of icing. (Remember to remove these before serving the cake!)

14. Place the parasol behind the sitting bear.

15. Finish off the enchanting scene by piping a layer of stars around the bottom edge of the cake.

34 TEDDY'S PICNIC

SETTING THE SCENE

An EXTREME-ly enjoyable party that will have the guests begging for more.

- Before finalizing the party details, visit the skateboard park that you intend using and view the facilities. Confirm the rules and regulations and find out if they have facilities for treating minor injuries.
- Speak to the park supervisor to ascertain the best time for a party and whether they allow snacks.
- It is mandatory that all children wear a helmet. Other safety gear should be encouraged where available. If children don't have their own skateboards, arrange that they can share with those who have.
- Ensure that you have safe and reliable transport for the number of guests that you intend to invite.
- Encourage guests to be punctual so that you may leave for the skateboard park at the stipulated time.
- Prepare a cooler bag with light refreshments, such as sandwiches and plenty of cold drinks (see also page 40), so that the children may have something to nibble and to quench their thirst at the park.
- Take a camera to the venue to capture the action.
- Predetermine the time that will be spent at the park and adhere to it, despite the pleas that you may receive for extra time.
- As this party will take the form of an outing to a skateboarding park, it is not necessary to do too much in the way of décor at home. Use red curling ribbon to tie a bunch of red balloons to the front gate so that guests will easily identify the birthday boy's home.
- Cover the party table with red crepe paper. Tie bundles of red balloons in the corners of the room and paste posters of skateboarding heroes on the walls.
- Once back home, the children can enjoy the birthday cake and party food. Thereafter allow them to relax by viewing a skateboarding video while they wait for their parents to fetch them.

Recommended age group: 8–12

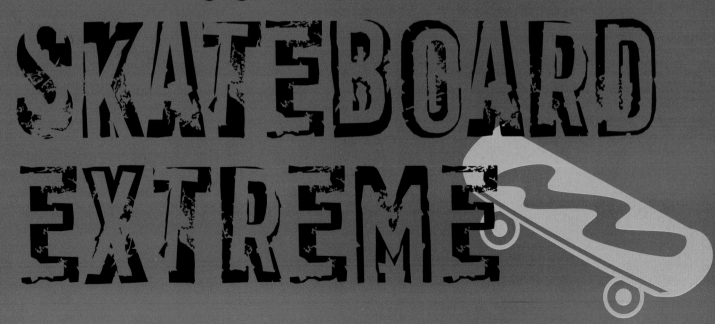

SKATEBOARD EXTREME

INVITATIONS

YOU WILL NEED:
Skateboard template (page 163)
Pencil
Red stiff board
Gold glitter pen
Gold beads
Craft glue

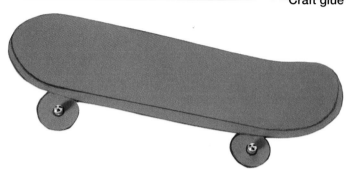

1. Use the template to trace the skateboard onto the stiff board, and then cut out the shape.
2. Write the invitation details (see Suggested Wording) on the back of the skateboard.
3. Use the glitter pen to write the guest's name on the front of the skateboard.
4. Attach the beads to the wheels with glue.

SUGGESTED WORDING
'Kickflip', 'Carve' and 'Ollie' at (child's name)'s party!
Move and manoeuvre at: (skateboarding park's name) on (date)
Transport departs from: (home address) at (time) sharp!
'Noseslide' back at: (time party ends)
RSVP: (Name) at (phone number) by (date)
Please bring skateboard and helmet.

TREAT BAGS

YOU WILL NEED:
Skateboarding toys
Small cake boxes
Prestik® or Blu-tac™
Glitter pen
Red curling ribbon

1. Attach the toy to the lid of the box with Prestik®.
2. Write the guest's name on the lid with glitter pen.
3. Tie curling ribbon around the box and through the toy to secure. (An alternative to the toy is to duplicate the invitation template and attach the cutout to the lid of the box.)

EXTREME MANŒUVRES CAKE

You will need to make a support that allows the cake to be raised above the table with the wheels underneath.

FOR THE CAKE SUPPORT (TEMPLATE, PAGE 163):

Handsaw or jigsaw

1 x plywood board, 3–5 mm thick,
   measuring 150 mm wide x 500 mm long

2 x 20 mm thick blocks of pine,
   each measuring 75 mm square

1 x 20 mm thick block of pine,
   measuring 20 mm wide x 75 mm long

Wood glue

6 mm diameter wooden dowel, cut into
   4 x 35 mm long pieces

1. Use the saw to shape each end of the 500 mm length of hardboard.
2. Place the square 75 mm blocks about 120 mm from each end of the underside of the board, and attach to the centre of the width with wood glue.
3. Place the smaller block upright in the centre to prevent sagging and glue in position.
4. Drill a 6 mm diameter hole 10 mm deep into each side of the square blocks, 32 mm from the base.
5. Sharpen one end of each dowel and insert the blunt end into the hole to support the wheels.

FOR THE CAKE:

2 x Basic Cake (page 160) – two x 300 x 240 mm

Icing (page 160) – red, white

Star-shaped cookie cutter (the birthday child may wish to design a unique emblem for the board instead of a star – encourage this personal contribution!)

White star-shaped sweets

4 x red Smarties®

Gold balls

1. Bake the cakes as directed and leave to cool completely.
2. Cut out and assemble the cakes on the prepared board according to the templates.
3. Use some of the offcuts to build the cake up slightly at each end to provide a slightly upturned contour to the overall shape of the skateboard.
4. Coat the skateboard with red icing.
5. Outline a star shape in the centre of the board with the cookie cutter, or use your child's preferred emblem, and use the star nozzle and white icing to decorate.
6. Pipe a row of white stars near the front end of the board and use the star sweets to enhance.
7. Coat the wheels with white icing and place in position so that the dowel rods support them.
8. Place Smarties® in the centre of each wheel and surround with gold balls.

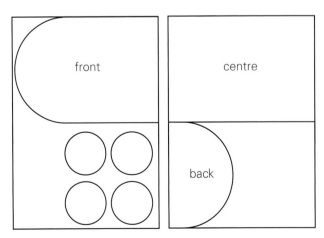

PARTY FOOD

GRINDING ALONG

Party Cupcakes (page 161)
Gold foil cookie cups (baking cases)
Icing (page 160) – red
Skateboard sweets
Plastic dolls (optional)
Gold balls

1. Bake the cupcakes in the cookie cups according to the recipe. Leave to cool completely.
2. Cover the top of the cakes with red icing and place the skateboard sweet in the centre.
3. Add a dab of icing to the sweet and attach the doll to the skateboard, if using.
4. Arrange the gold balls on the cupcake to decorate.

WINNER'S JUICE

Plastic juice bottles
Toy medal party favours
Fresh fruit juice
Prestik® or Blu-tac™

1. Fill the bottles with juice.
2. Drape the medal around the bottle, using a blob of Prestik® to secure.

SKATEBOARD BISCUITS

Easy Biscuits (page 161)
Skateboard template (page 163)
Stiff cardboard
Sour liquorice ropes
Icing (page 160) – red, white
White star-shaped sweets

1. Prepare the biscuit dough as per the recipe.
2. Trace the template onto the cardboard, cut it out and use to cut out the biscuits. Bake as directed and leave to cool completely.
3. Cut two pieces of liquorice rope to fit across the underside of the board for the wheels. Dab icing on the underside of the biscuit and fix the wheels in position.
4. Coat the top of the biscuit with red icing.
5. Use the writing nozzle to decorate the skateboard with a few white icing dots and place the star sweet in position.

SPARE WHEELS

Ready-made mini swiss rolls
Icing (page 160) – white
Red Mini Smarties®
Gold balls

1. Cut each swiss roll in half and coat the cut ends with white icing.
2. Place a mini Smartie® in the centre and surround with the gold balls as illustrated.

SETTING THE SCENE

A sleepover is always a recipe for success and when your favourite fashion doll is included in the glamour parade, sweet dreams are sure to ensue!

* Half-fill brown paper packets with damp sea sand and place a candle in each. Place these in two neat rows to create a walkway to the front door. (Always maintain supervision whenever candles are used.)

* Cover the party table with purple crepe paper with ruched lilac organza material over the top. Scatter lilac silk flowers and shredded glitter foil over the table. Place any fashion dolls that you may have on the party table, as well as throughout the house.

* Create a canopy above the table with purple and lilac twisted streamers draped from the centre of the ceiling to the outer edges. Cut out cardboard stars (see template, page 162), spray with lilac and purple craft spray and suspend above the table with fishing line. Decorate with glitter glue.

* Twirl varying lengths of lilac and purple curling ribbon and suspend from the ceiling above the table. Attach posters of your child's favourite doll to the walls. Drape fairy lights around mirrors.

* As the overnight guests will spend time in the bathroom, it is important to continue the décor into this room as well. Attach purple and lilac balloons, tied together with curling ribbon, to a strategic corner. Cascade strips of purple and lilac curling ribbon down the walls and around the mirror. Use small bowls of fresh or silk flowers in shades to match, and position a doll to keep an eye on proceedings.

* The slumber room should also be decorated and it is advisable to empty the area of furniture, if possible. Attach glow-in-the-dark stars to the ceiling and purple and lilac balloons to the corners of the room.

* Place a low table in the centre of the room and cover with a purple cloth. This may be used as the changing table for the dolls and should include dolls' clothes as well as fashion accessories. Guests will play till the wee hours of the morning!

* Arrange the sleeping bags in this room while the guests are being entertained and place a treat bag on each pillow so that they may have a midnight feast! Provide a torch for the children to use should they require it during the night.

Recommended age group: 8–12

Funky Fashion Sleepover!

INVITATIONS

YOU WILL NEED (PER INVITATION):
1 x strip of lilac notepaper (200 x 70 mm),
to fit shoe when folded
Pen
1 x plastic miniature fashion shoe
Purple curling ribbon
Felt-tip marker

1. Write the invitation details on the notepaper (see Suggested Wording), fold up and place inside the shoe.
2. Wind the curling ribbon around the shoe and knot at the top.
3. Write the guest's name on the sole of the shoe with the felt-tip marker.

SUGGESTED WORDING
Step onto the catwalk and join (child's name)'s birthday bash on (date)
With the House of: (surname) at (address)
Duration of extravaganza: (time from start to finish)
RSVP: Fashion co-ordinator at (phone number) by (date)
Dress: As your favourite fashion doll!
Bring: Your favourite fashion doll, pyjamas, sleeping bag, pillow, and personal toiletries

TREAT BAGS

YOU WILL NEED:
Small cake boxes
Felt-tip marker
Purple paper doilies
Craft glue
Small mirrors
Prestik® or Blu-tac™
Purple or lilac curling ribbon

1. Write the guest's name on the side of the box.
2. Glue the doily to the lid of the box.
3. Secure the mirror to the centre of the doily with a small blob of Prestik®. Tie the ribbon around the box, knotting it over the mirror as illustrated.

GAMES AND ACTIVITIES

Provide work stations* where the guests will be able to:
– Apply make-up such as lip gloss and eye shadow.
– Receive manicures with funky shades of nail polish and nail tattoos. Remember to include an emery board.
– Apply temporary tattoos, body paints and glitters.
– Accessorize their hair with hairpieces, gels, hair glitters and wash-out coloured hair sprays.
– Dress up with clothes and accessories such as beads, boas, bags, high-heeled shoes, and so on.
– Dress their dolls with a change of clothes and accessories. Make provision for children who haven't brought a doll.
– Remove all traces of make-up and nail polish before bedtime. Some children may wish to retain their pretty fingernails until a later stage.

*For practical reasons these stations should not be included in the sleeping area.

Divide the children into pairs so that they may assist each other at the beauty stations – consider this when planning invitations so that you may have an even number of children. Recruit a friend to assist with the supervision of the work stations. (Obtain parents' permission for the application of make-up and check for allergies!)

Activity 1

Divide the girls into pairs and allow them to move through the work stations, excluding the final one, of course, which contains the make-up removers. To ensure an easy flow of movement, number the stations so that the girls visit them in consecutive order – have each pair draw a number from a hat to determine their starting point. The time spent at each station is according to a preset limit.

At each work station the pair assists each other with make-up, hair, manicures, and so on. Allow sufficient time so that they don't have to rush through the pampering. Provide sufficient towels and capes, together with paper towels to mop up any spills. Maintain a continuous supply of their favourite music throughout the proceedings.

Activity 2

Mark out a catwalk for the fashion parade by placing two parallel strips of masking tape on the floor. Place chairs on either side for the audience. A toy echo microphone may be used by the Master of Ceremonies (same friend as from the work station supervision!), who will announce each girl and allow her to move up and down the catwalk in time to the beat of the background music. When each child has paraded, prizes are awarded in categories that will ensure that each child receives one, for example: Curliest Hair, Cutest Tattoo, Biggest Smile.

Be sure to record the fashion parade on camera so that they may watch it from their sleeping bags!

In addition to the single parade the girls may wish to plan some choreography together in pairs or as a group.

Activity 3

Display the guests' dolls on a table and award prizes as above. Ensure that every doll receives a prize.

Pass the Pillow

Game to signal the start of slumber preparations:

YOU WILL NEED
1 x small pillow or cushion
Music

The girls sit in a circle and pass the pillow from one to the other as the music plays. When the music stops, the girl holding the pillow is eliminated and has to move to the last work station where she has to remove her make-up and prepare for bed! The game continues in this manner until one child is left. She receives a prize before moving on to the cleansing work station. When the rest of the girls have cleaned up, they receive tokens.

Activity 4

Provide videos for slumber-time viewing. (If you recorded the fashion parade, now's the time to show it!)

PARTY FOOD

Supper

Pasta is always a good choice. Another option is chicken drumsticks and vegetable kebabs (mushrooms, cocktail tomatoes, cucumber and pineapple chunks), served with tomato sauce, mustard and chutney, with cheesy cocktail rolls on the side.

Supermodels

Small sweets of choice
Wafer ice-cream cones
Marie biscuits or Rich Tea™ biscuits
Icing (page 160) – lilac, purple, yellow
Sugar paste, or gumball if preferred
Star-shaped sweets
Pipe cleaners – 100 mm lengths
Fine craft brush
Red food colouring
Silver balls

1. Place the sweets of choice in the ice-cream cone.
2. Coat one side of a Marie biscuit with icing and place, iced side down, over the open end of the cone. Upend so that the biscuit forms the base. Cut the tip off the cone, and discard.
3. For the head, roll some sugar paste into a ball and attach to the open end of the cone with icing.
4. For the clothes, use the star nozzle to pipe two rows of four stars across the front of the cone at the doll's waist. Pipe the trousers at a slight angle. A pyramid of stars creates the bodice: three at the waist, two above, finishing with one just below the head.
5. Mould two pieces of sugar paste to attach to the end of each leg for the foot, or pipe a white star.
6. Use the star nozzle, yellow icing and a pull-out motion to create the hair. Attach a star-shaped sweet.
7. Gently insert the pipe cleaners in position on either side of the bodice for arms, and bend to shape.
8. Wet the brush and use to dissolve a pinch of food colouring to paint the mouth. Attach silver balls for the eyes using a small dab of icing to secure.
9. Pipe a row of stars around the base of the cone to neaten, and enhance the doll with silver balls.

Glowing Mudpacks

Instant chocolate pudding (1 packet serves 6)
125 ml clear plastic containers with lids
Lilac and purple curling ribbon, about 240 mm of each per pudding
Prestik® or Blu-tac™
Glow-in-the-dark tokens, or stickers if preferred

1. Prepare the pudding according to directions and pour 100 ml into each container. Set in the fridge.
2. Lay two strips of curling ribbon on top of each other, attach a dab of Prestik® to their midpoint and attach to the lid. Use Prestik® to secure the token on top of the ribbons. Place the lids on the containers.

Lucky Lips

Easy Biscuits (page 161)
Lips template (page 162)
Icing (page 160) – purple, red, lilac, pink

1. Prepare the biscuit dough as per the recipe.
2. Trace the template onto cardboard and use it to cut out the biscuits. Bake and leave to cool completely.
3. Coat each biscuit with a different colour icing. Use a toothpick to differentiate the upper and lower lips.

Starry Night Cream

Glow-in-the-dark stars
Long-handled plastic spoons
Prestik® or Blu-tac™
Lilac and purple curling ribbon, about 150 mm of each per treat
Ice cream – lilac or purple (colour softened ice cream with powdered food colouring)
Plastic parfait glasses
Star-shaped sweets

1. Attach the star to the spoon handle with Prestik®. Tie the two ribbons in a knot around the handle.
2. Place two scoops of ice cream in the glass, sprinkle with star sweets and place the spoon in position.

LIVING DOLL BIRTHDAY CAKE

This lovely lady needs a lot of space on the party table!

2½ x Basic Cake (page 160) – Two x 300 x 240 mm
   cakes; one x 200 mm round cake
Icing (page 160) – flesh-coloured, lilac, purple,
   brown, red, black, white
Heart-shaped cookie cutter
Black liquorice strap
Large silver balls
Grape-flavoured jelly twists
Eye template (page 164)
Lips template (page 162)
Red edible glitter
Ready-made icing flower for hair, or as preferred

1. Bake the cakes according to the recipe and leave
    to cool completely. Cut out and assemble the
    cakes according to the templates, flipping the arms
    upside down and placing them so that they appear
    akimbo. Use the round cake for the head.

2. Coat the face, neck, arms, mid-riff and feet with
    flesh-coloured icing. Use the star nozzle to create
    the clothes and pipe as illustrated. Use a cookie
    cutter to outline a heart shape on the top.

3. Place a liquorice strap in position for a belt and
    embellish with silver balls. Make a pocket chain
    with silver balls. Pipe a row of purple stars around
    one wrist and enhance with silver balls.

4. Pipe the soles of the shoes with brown icing and
    create the shoe thongs with the jelly twists.
    Decorate with an iced purple star and a silver ball.

5. Use the eye and lip templates as a guide for the
    facial features. Use a writing nozzle to outline the
    mouth and eyes with black icing. Create eyelashes
    and dot a beauty spot on the cheek.

6. Colour the eyes as illustrated, using the writing
    nozzle and spreading the icing where necessary
    using a toothpick. Fill in the lips with the star nozzle
    and sprinkle with edible glitter.

7. Use the star nozzle, brown icing and a pull-out
    action to create the hair. Adorn with a flower.

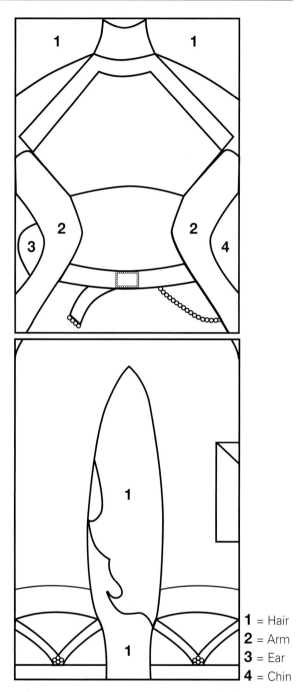

1 = Hair
2 = Arm
3 = Ear
4 = Chin

For Breakfast the Following Morning

Lay out a self-service spread consisting of: crumpets,
syrup, muffins, jams, fresh cream, a selection of
seasonal fruits, flavoured yoghurts and fresh fruit juice.

SETTING THE SCENE

Strike a hit when you host this party and be the most popular parent on the block – both boys and girls will be enthralled!

- Contact the bowling alley beforehand to establish their criteria and to confirm a booking on the date required. Plan to have the party food either before or after the outing, depending on the time scheduled at the alley. If the latter is the preferred option, ascertain whether you may take light refreshments to the venue, in which case it is wise to pack a drink for each child together with a light snack.
- Take a camera to the venue so that you may capture the action.
- Although the greater portion of this party will be held at the bowling alley, children will appreciate the following simple yet effective home décor.
- Cut out a large bowling ball from cardboard, paint it red and include three black finger holes. Mount the bowling ball on the front gate together with a bunch of red, black and white balloons that have been tied together with red, black and white curling ribbon.
- Duplicate the cardboard bowling balls in varying sizes and use the smaller balls to lay a trail from the gate to the front entrance. Use the others to mount on the walls in the party area.
- Cover the party table with white crepe paper and add red and black cardboard balls and red and black confetti to complete the effect.
- Create a canopy above the party table by draping twisted red, black and white streamers from the centre of the ceiling to the outer edges.
- Attach bundles of red, black and white balloons to the corners of the ceiling.

Recommended age group: 10-12

TENPIN BOWLING

INVITATIONS

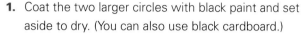

YOU WILL NEED (PER INVITATION):

1 x cardboard circle, 105 mm in diameter
1 x cardboard circle, 35 mm in diameter
Black non-toxic craft spray
Notepaper of choice
Red and black curling ribbon
Prestik® or Blu-tac™
3 x small red paper circles, 8 mm in diameter
Craft glue
Paper punch
3 x small red paper circles, 5 mm in diameter
Glitter pen

1. Coat the two larger circles with black paint and set aside to dry. (You can also use black cardboard.)
2. Write the invitation details (see Suggested Wording) on the notepaper. Fold and tie with curling ribbon. Attach to the back of the largest ball with Prestik® so that it is not visible from the front.
3. Glue the three 8 mm circles onto the large ball and punch a hole near the edge.
4. Write the guest's name at the back of the 35 mm circle with the glitter pen.
5. Glue the three 5 mm circles to this ball, punch a hole near the edge, and attach to the larger ball with the curling ribbon.

SUGGESTED WORDING

Score a strike at (child's name)'s party on (date)
Bowling house: (address)
Curve ball delivery: (time party starts)
Dead ball delivery: (time party ends)
RSVP: The House Manager at (phone number) by (date)
Dress: As for tenpin bowling – (provide details of the outing here) (You may suggest that the guests dress in red, white or black.)

TREAT BAGS

YOU WILL NEED (PER BAG):

1 x cardboard circle, 105 mm in diameter
1 x cardboard circle, 35 mm in diameter
Black non-toxic craft spray
3 x small red paper circles, 8 mm in diameter
Craft glue
1 x red gift bag
Glitter pen

3 x small red paper circles, 5 mm in diameter
Paper punch
Red and black curling ribbon

1. Coat the two larger circles with black paint and set aside to dry.
2. Glue the three red 8 mm circles to the largest ball and glue the ball to the centre front of the bag.
3. Write the guest's name at the back of the 35 mm circle with the glitter pen.
4. Glue the three 5 mm circles to this ball and punch a hole near the edge. Attach this nametag to the handle with the curling ribbon.

AWESOME ALLEY CAKE

1 x Basic Cake (page 160) – 300 x 240 mm
Icing (page 160) – white
150 g sugar paste
Red powdered food colouring
1 x wafer biscuit, cut into 3 x 15 mm wide strips
2 x toy plastic tenpin bowling sets
Black non-toxic food colouring pen
3 x red gumballs or use red sugar paste
   to mould balls
2 x dolls

1. Bake the cake according to the recipe and leave to cool completely.
2. Coat the top and sides of the cake with white icing.
3. Use a toothpick and a ruler to mark four gutters – about 15 mm wide – along the length of the cake as illustrated. (The space between the two centre gutters measures about 15 mm wide as well.)
4. Colour the sugar paste with the red food colouring. Roll out the sugar paste to 2–4 mm thick on a surface dusted with icing sugar and so that it measures about 320 x 80 mm. Cut four strips measuring 320 x 15 mm and place in position on the cake. Trim the edges to neaten.
5. Sandwich the three wafer strips together with icing to make a stand for the bowling balls. Coat with icing and place between the central gutters.
6. Use the star nozzle to decorate the central gutter and pipe a row of stars around the top edge of the cake as well as around the base.
7. Place the pins at one end of each alley.
8. Mark the gumballs with the black pen to create finger holes and place two balls on the stand and one in the alley.
9. Place a doll in each alley.

PARTY FOOD

A SWEET STRIKE!

Easy Biscuits (page 161)
Pin template (page 162)
Icing (page 160) – white, red
Black non-toxic food colouring pen (or black
   powdered food colouring dissolved in water
   or white alcohol)
Red gumball

1. Prepare the biscuit dough as per the recipe.
2. Trace the template onto stiff paper, cut it out and
   use this pin to cut out the biscuits. Bake as directed
   and leave to cool completely.
3. Coat the biscuit with white icing and use a writing
   nozzle to make two red stripes at the 'neck' of
   the pin.
4. Draw or paint three black dots on the gumball and
   place at the base of the biscuit, pressing lightly into
   the icing to secure.

BOWL ME OVER SURPRISE

Wafer cookie cups
Small sweets of choice
Marie biscuits or Rich Tea™ biscuits
Icing (page 160) – white
White curling ribbon
Toy plastic bowling pins – one per treat
Silver balls

1. Fill the cookie cup with sweets.
2. Coat the Marie biscuit with icing and place over
   the open end of the cookie cup. Upend so that
   the biscuit forms the base.
3. Use the star nozzle to decorate the flat top of the
   cookie cup and pipe a row of stars around the base
   to neaten.
4. Tie a short length of curling ribbon around the 'neck'
   of the bowling pin and place in position on top of the
   cookie cup.
5. Enhance with silver balls.

WINNING BALL CUPCAKES

Party Cupcakes (page 161)
Red paper or foil cookie cups (baking cases)
Icing (page 160) – white
Small round red sweets

1. Bake the cupcakes in the cookie cups as per the
   recipe and leave to cool completely.
2. Use a serrated knife to trim into a ball shape if
   necessary before covering the top of the cupcake
   with white icing.
3. Add the three red sweets as illustrated.

A COOL BALL

Black non-toxic food colouring pen
Gumballs
Ice cream
Wafer ice cream cones or plastic parfait dishes
Wafer fans

1. Mark three holes on the gumball with the pen.
2. Place a generous scoop of ice cream in the cone or
   parfait dish, top with a gumball and enhance with
   the wafer fan.

Witches &

SETTING THE SCENE

Witches and wizards will be spellbound with these ideas and will certainly be waving their wands for more! This theme can easily be adapted for a Halloween party.

★ Tie purple and gold balloons to the front gate with purple and gold curling ribbon. Cut out huge spiders (see template, page 164) from black cardboard and lay a trail from the front gate to the entrance.

★ Suspend a fake cobweb in the doorway and position a gigantic plastic spider to welcome guests. Lean a witches broom against the doorframe.

★ Cover the party table with purple crepe paper and arrange plastic snakes, bats, frogs and spiders on the table, and throughout the party area. Cut out cardboard moons, stars and lightning bolts (see templates, pages 162, 164), spray with gold non-toxic craft spray, brush with gold glitter and scatter on the table.

★ Create a canopy above the party table by twisting purple streamers and draping them from the centre of the ceiling to the outer edges. Suspend plastic bats and spiders from the ceiling with fishing line so that they hang over the party table at varying heights. Intersperse with suspended lightning bolts. Cascade purple streamers vertically down the walls, interspersed with a few ropes of gold tinsel. Tie bundles of purple and gold balloons together with purple and gold curling ribbon and attach to the corners of the ceiling. Line windows in the party area with purple cellophane to create an eerie effect.

★ Use cardboard to make a large black cauldron (see template, page 164) to mount on the main wall in the party area. Brush with streaks of gold glitter glue. Coat polystyrene balls of varying sizes with non-toxic green craft paint; glue them onto cardboard backing and position above the cauldron to create a 'bubbling froth' in the pot. Lastly attach a few plastic snakes, frogs, spiders and bats to the frothing bubbles with small dabs of Prestik® or Blu-tac™.

★ Serve food from cauldrons and drape large jellied snakes over the edge. Food may also be served from cardboard rounds, sprayed gold with non-toxic spray. Attach a plastic mouse, spider or frog to each.

★ Sprinkle feathers in varying shades of purple on the floor and randomly throughout the house.

★ Parents and helpers should don fancy dress to add to the enchantment!

Recommended age group: 6–12

Wizards

INVITATIONS

YOU WILL NEED:

8 mm-diameter dowel sticks – about 220 mm long
Black non-toxic craft spray
Craft glue
Gold glitter
Witch's hat template (page 164)
Pencil
Cardboard
Scissors
Small witch motif or self-adhesive gold stars (optional)
Paper punch
Purple notepaper
Gold curling ribbon

1. Coat the dowel stick with the craft spray and set aside to dry. Coat 30 mm at one end of the dry stick with craft glue and sprinkle with glitter.
2. Trace the witch's hat onto the cardboard, cut out and paint black. Write the guest's name on the back of the hat and attach the witch motif/gold stars to the front. Punch a hole near the tip of the hat.
3. Write the invitation details (see Suggested Wording) on the notepaper, fold around the wand and tie with curling ribbon. Thread the ribbon through the hole in the hat and knot to secure.

SUGGESTED WORDING

Be a part of the hocus-pocus at (child's name)'s birthday party on (date).
Mount your broom and fly over to: (address)
Wave your wand to cast spells from: (time party starts) to (time party ends)
RSVP: The Resident Witch at (phone number) by (date)
Dress: As a witch or wizard. Bring your invitation wand!

TREAT BAGS

YOU WILL NEED (PER BAG):

1 x 2-litre plastic soft drink container
Craft scissors
Black non-toxic craft spray
Paper punch
1 x 300 mm-long gold pipe cleaner
Self-adhesive gold stars
Black and gold curling ribbon – cut into 500–600 mm lengths
Witch's hat template (page 164)
Pencil
Cardboard
Gold glitter pen

1. Cut the upper section from the container and discard. Paint the container black and set aside.
2. Mark points around the rim of the dry container – about 20 mm apart and 5 mm from the edge. Using the points as a guide, carefully punch holes through each marked point.
3. Insert the ends of the pipe cleaner through two opposite holes and twist the ends upwards towards the rim of the container so that the pipe cleaner forms a handle. Attach the stars to the container.
4. Fold each length of ribbon in half, insert the loop through the hole and make a knot by feeding the tail ends through the loop and pulling to secure.
5. Trace the template onto the cardboard, cut out, paint black and set aside to dry. Stick stars onto the hat.
6. Punch a hole near the tip of the hat, write the guest's name on the hat and attach to the handle with gold ribbon.

GAMES AND ACTIVITIES

Ride the Broom

YOU WILL NEED (PER TEAM):

1 x witches' broomstick
1 x polystyrene ball

Divide the children into two or more teams and have them line up one behind the other. On starter's orders, the first child in each team must place the ball on the ground and, using the broom, they must guide the ball to a predetermined point away from the team.

After successfully arriving at the point, they must pick up the ball, mount the broom and 'fly' back to their team, where the broom and ball are handed to the next child. The game continues in the same manner until all the children have completed the task. The winning team receives a prize, the rest receive tokens.

Climbing Haunted Hill

YOU WILL NEED (PER TEAM):

Cardboard discs, one colour per team, and as many
    as preferred for the course
1 x list of clues for the location of the discs
Prize tokens as per the rewards

Number each disc and write instructions for forfeits or rewards underneath. Examples: 'Meet wicked wizard on path, run and hide for 2 minutes'; 'Potion not working, wait at this point for 2 minutes'; 'Find a broom and hitch a ride – choose a token'; 'Bitten by witch's snake – hop on one leg to next point'; 'The wizard has made your feet disappear, crawl to next point'; 'Magic wand waves you past next token without stopping'. Place the discs on the ground before the start of the game. Divide the children into two or more teams and allocate a colour to each team (the colours should correspond with the colours chosen for the discs). Each team should receive the same instructions, but should start at different points. Each team must move from their first base point to the next, each time waiting for the entire team to arrive before moving on to the next point. The first team to finish receives a prize, the rest receive tokens.

Undo the Bad Magic!

Tell the children that a wicked wizard has cast a spell that has changed each of them into an animal or insect and it's up to them to break the spell!

YOU WILL NEED:

1 x sticker for each child bearing the name and a
    drawing of an animal or insect
1 x list for each child containing all the animals/
    insects that have been allocated to the children
1 x pencil for each child
1 x wand
1 x container of prizes – one for each child

Have the children line up and attach a sticker to their backs. They must not divulge the name of the sticker to the wearer, as each child has to ascertain their own description by a process of elimination. Give each child a list and a pencil and, on starter's orders, they must look at the stickers on the backs of the rest of the children and eliminate that particular creature from their list. Once they have established their identity by eliminating everyone else from their list, they must sit down. When all the children are seated, the game leader (the Good Witch) asks each child in turn to call out his or her identity. If they are correct the Good Witch waves the wand and the spell is broken! The children may then select a prize.

A Freezing Spell

YOU WILL NEED:

1 x wand
Music

The caller determines the action that the children must perform on the wave of the wand each time the music starts, for example: 'Fly like a bat', 'Hop like a frog', 'Run like a mouse'. When the music stops, the children must freeze in position. The last child to freeze is eliminated and must stay frozen to the spot. The game continues until one child is left. The winner receives a prize, the rest receive a token.

PARTY FOOD

Levitating Beasties

Party Cupcakes (page 161)
Gold foil cookie cups (baking cases)
Icing (page 160) – dark purple
Gold balls
Small plastic toy rats or similar creatures
Prestik® or Blu-tac™
Clear plastic cocktail sticks

1. Bake the cupcakes in the cookie cups as per the recipe and leave to cool completely.
2. Coat the cupcakes with the icing and decorate with the gold balls.
3. Attach the chosen critter to the blunt end of the cocktail stick using a blob of Prestik®.
4. Insert the sharp end of the cocktail stick into the cupcake so that the mouse 'levitates'.

Freaky Fingers

Easy Biscuits (page 161)
Icing (page 160) – flesh-coloured
Wooden skewers
Flaked almonds

1. Prepare the biscuit dough as per the recipe.
2. Cut the biscuits into finger shapes (use your own finger as a template!) and gently insert a wooden skewer into the bottom end of each. Bake as directed and leave to cool completely.
3. Coat with icing and make the wrinkles and lines with a toothpick.
4. Attach a flaked almond onto the pointed end to resemble a fingernail.

Creepy Crystal Balls

Wafer cookie cups
Small sweets of choice
Marie biscuits or Rich Tea™ biscuits
Icing (page 160) – white, purple
Gold balls
Black plastic toy spiders, or as preferred
Small plastic spheres

1. Fill the cookie cup with sweets.
2. Coat a Marie biscuit with icing and place over the cookie cup to cover. Upend so that the biscuit forms the base.
3. Cover the cookie cup with white icing and use the star nozzle with purple icing to pipe a row of stars around the base. Enhance with gold balls.
4. Place a toy spider in the sphere and position the sphere on top of the cookie cup.

Pickled Toads

Black and purple curling ribbon – 100 mm lengths
Prestik® or Blu-tac™
125 ml clear plastic containers with lids
Toy plastic toads, or as preferred, to fit into container
Pale yellow jelly (powder or cubes)
  (1 packet serves 5–6)

1. Attach black and purple curling ribbon to the lid of the container with a small blob of Prestik®. Set aside.
2. Wash and disinfect the toy toads and place inside the plastic containers.
3. Mix the jelly according to the packet instructions and gently pour into the container until it covers the frog. Place in the fridge to set.
4. Seal the container with the lid before serving.

HAUNTED HOUSE CAKE

2 x Basic Cake (page 160) – 4 x 200 mm square cakes
1 x Basic Cake (page 160) – 3 x ±750 g food cans
Icing (page 160) – dark purple
Wooden skewers
Clear plastic cylindrical container – 100 x 60 mm
2 x toy witches
2 x wafer ice-cream cones
Black edible glitter
3 x large gold balls

500 g sugar paste
Powdered food colouring – black, yellow
Door and ghost templates (page 164)
Black non-toxic food marking pen
Liquorice cables
Black toy spiders, bats, ghosts, and so on
Florist's wire
Black artificial spiders' web

1. Prepare the cake batter as directed. To make the square cakes, pour the batter into the tins, adding slightly more batter into one tin so that one layer can be slightly thicker than the rest – this will be used for the roof. Bake as directed and leave to cool completely.

2. To make the turret sections of the cake, divide the batter between the lined and greased food cans so that they are three-quarters full. Bake as directed and leave to cool completely.

3. Place three of the square cakes on top of each other and sandwich together with icing to form the house. Coat the top with icing. Cut the thicker fourth layer diagonally across to form four triangles. Place the triangles in position alongside each other, longest side down, and sandwich them together with icing so that they fit neatly on top of the house to form the roof. Coat the entire cake with dark purple icing and use the tip of a knife to create a rough plastered appearance on the walls.

4. Cut one of the turrets in half widthwise and use to lengthen the two remaining turrets. Join the sections with icing and support with wooden skewers if necessary. Secure the turrets on either side of the house with skewers.

5. Hollow out a section from the centre top of one of the turrets to accommodate the cylindrical container. Cover the lower half of the witch's body with foil and place in the container. Gently insert into the hollowed-out section of the tower so that the uncovered part of the witch peers out. Coat the turrets with purple icing to match the house.

6. Fill in and neaten the section around the container. Coat the top of the container with icing and use the star nozzle to pipe two rows of stars around the edge of the container.

7. Coat the wafer cones with icing and sprinkle with black glitter. Place in position on the top of each turret. Add a large gold ball to the tip of the turret to enhance.

8. Set aside a small ball of sugar paste and colour the rest dark grey or black. Roll out a small piece to 2–4 mm thick on a surface dusted with icing sugar and use the template, enlarged slightly, to cut out a door. Remove the top centre section of the door and place the door in position on the house. Add a gold ball for the doorknob.

9. Cut three 40 mm squares for the windows. Create four windowpanes in each window frame by cutting out circles using the back of a small icing nozzle. Attach two windows to the house and one to one of the turrets.

10. Halve the leftover sugar paste and roll out one section. Use the template to cut out a ghost. Pierce the eye sockets with a wooden skewer and fix the ghost to the opening in the door, trimming the edges to fit if necessary.

11. Colour the remaining sugar paste yellow and roll out. Use a drinking straw to punch out circles. Shape the circles into eyes and make a dot on each with the food marking pen for the pupils. Paste pairs into the windowpanes.

12. Roll out the rest of the black or dark grey sugar paste, working with small balls at a time, and cut out 20 mm squares. Use these blocks to tile the roof as shown.

13. Cut the liquorice cables into 15 mm lengths and attach to the base of the house and turrets as illustrated.

14. Attach toys as preferred, using wooden skewers and florist's wire, so that some hover about the roof.

15. Drape the spider's web over the cake. (Take care if you are using candles – keep flames away from the web!)

SETTING THE SCENE

All boys enjoy a night out and dads and other male family members will have just as much fun at this party as their exuberant charges. (As with all children's' parties, adult supervision is essential throughout the duration of this event, and careful consideration should be given to the location of the candles and campfire.)

* Use garden candles to light a path from the front gate to the party area.

* Either have one large tent or sufficient smaller ones to accommodate all the guests, as well as the supervising adults. Decorate the outside of the tent/s with balloons and streamers in camouflage shades. Cut out cardboard stars and moons, paint with glow-in-the-dark paint and attach to the outside as well as the inside of the tent/s with Prestik® or Blu-tac™. Suspend the rest in the garden trees and shrubs with fishing line. Alternatively, use plastic glow-in-the-dark shapes if preferred.

* Place plastic/rubber snakes, spiders and other creepy crawlies throughout the party area. Arrange washed stones and pebbles on the table to provide hiding places for creepy crawlies.

* String party lights in the trees or against the house. Play tapes of animal and bird sounds.

* Cover the party table with camouflage fabric and top with a layer of clear plastic to protect against spills, particularly as the table will be used for serving breakfast as well.

* Create a canopy above the party table with twisted streamers in camouflage colours by draping them from the centre of the ceiling to the corners. Cascade streamers vertically down the walls in the party area. Draw owls on poster paper, decorate with glow-in-the-dark paint and mount against the walls.

* Thread fishing line through the tails of large jellied snake sweets and suspend above the table. Make sure that there are sufficient for the number of guests, who will be able to 'capture' them.

* Once the guest list has been confirmed, divide the names into groups and allocate each group to an adult helper. Ask the birthday child to assist with names for each group that will fit with the theme, for example, Spitting Snakes, Stinging Scorpions, and so on. Make a sticker for each guest with his group name and a descriptive picture/drawing of the chosen topic. On arrival, the children are given their stickers and are introduced to their group leader, who will wear similar identification. This will facilitate supervision, especially for younger groups. Provide each group leader with a flashlight.

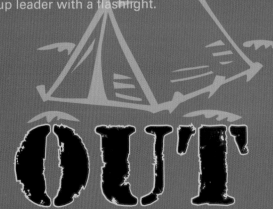

Recommended age group: 8–12

INVITATIONS

YOU WILL NEED (PER INVITATION):
Notepaper – 100 mm square
(colour of choice)
Gold glitter pen
Gold curling ribbon
1 x toy plastic flashlight
Star template (page 162)
Pencil
Board paper (colour to
match notepaper)
Scissors
Paper punch

1. Write the invitation details (see Suggested Wording) on the notepaper with the glitter pen. Fold the paper and tie it to the flashlight with the curling ribbon.
2. Trace the star onto the board paper, cut it out and write the guest's name on the star. Punch a hole near one point and thread the star onto the ribbon. Tie a knot to secure.

SUGGESTED WORDING
Experience the wild outdoors at (name)'s sleepover!
Tents will be pitched on: (date)
Camp site: (address)
Stars will twinkle from: … to … (duration of party)
RSVP: Camp Counsellor at (phone number) by (date)
Bring: Pyjamas, sleeping bag, pillow, personal toiletries and a flashlight

TREAT BAGS

YOU WILL NEED:
Small cake boxes
Black non-toxic craft spray
Prestik® or Blu-tac™
Glow-in-the-dark centipedes or other creatures
Gold glitter pen

1. Spray the cake box black and set aside to dry.
2. Use a small dab of Prestik® to attach the centipede to the lid of the box.
3. Write the guest's name on the bottom of the box with the gold glitter pen.

GAMES AND ACTIVITIES

SCAVENGER HUNT

YOU WILL NEED (PER TEAM):
1 x list of items to be collected
1 x container for the items collected

The extent of the list will depend on the party environment and how far the guests are allowed to venture (they should be under the supervision of their group leader). Try to enlist the co-operation of a few friendly neighbours to allow entry to their properties as well!

Leave envelopes containing clues along the route, clearly marked with the group's personal identity. Provide each group with a different order so that they won't all be at the same point simultaneously. Be as creative as circumstances dictate. The first successful team home wins a prize, the rest receive tokens.

FEED THE MONKEY

YOU WILL NEED:
Bananas – one for each pair of children
1 x blindfold for each child

Divide the children into pairs and provide each pair with two blindfolds and one banana. The blindfolded children must sit facing each other, with one of the pair holding the banana. On starter's orders, the child holding the banana must peel it carefully and then proceed to feed his hungry monkey who is squealing for food. One mouthful of banana should be taken at a time and a squeal indicates that the monkey is ready for more. The first team to finish wins a prize, the rest receive tokens.

MOON WALK

YOU WILL NEED:
Music
1 x round cardboard disc per guest, each bearing
   a different number
1 x container bearing slips of paper with
   corresponding numbers written on each

Place the discs in a circle. When the music starts, the children must hop from one disc to another. When the music stops a slip is drawn from the container and the child standing on the corresponding disc is eliminated and receives a token. Both the disc and the paper slip are discarded. Play continues in the same manner until there is a winner, who receives a prize.

SLEEPING BAG HOP

YOU WILL NEED (PER TEAM):
1 x sleeping bag, or similar bag

Divide the children into two or more teams and have them line up one behind the other at a starting point. The first child in each team must step into the sleeping bag. On starter's orders, he must hop to the finish line, step out of the bag, run backwards to his team and hand the bag to the next child, who repeats the procedure. The game continues in the same manner until all the children have had a turn. The winning team receives a prize, the rest receive tokens.

SNAKE HUNT

Finish off the evening with this game.

YOU WILL NEED:
Plastic snakes, sufficient for the number of guests,
   plus a few extra
Flashlights

Hide the snakes in the party area and allow the children to search for them. As each child locates a snake, he is applauded, handed his treat bag containing midnight snacks, and sent to prepare for bed!

PARTY FOOD

SUPPER

Cook an assortment of sausages on the barbecue and serve on rolls with tomato sauce and mustard.

Make mini salad kebabs: cocktail tomatoes, pineapple chunks and mushrooms on a mini wooden skewer.

Marshmallows on skewers for toasting over the fire (under strict adult supervision only).

SWAMPS ALIVE

Party Cupcakes (page 161)
Silver foil cookie cups (baking cases)
Icing (page 160) – brown, green
Jelly crocodile sweets
Small bone-shaped sweets

1. Bake the cupcakes in the foil cookie cups as per the recipe and leave to cool completely.
2. Cover the top of the cupcake with brown icing and place the crocodile sweet in the centre.
3. Use the star nozzle to pipe tufts of grass and add the bone-shaped sweets as illustrated.

NIGHT LIZARD

Wafer ice-cream cones
Small sweets of choice
Marie biscuits or Rich Tea™ biscuits
Icing (page 160) – brown
Glow-in-the-dark toy lizards
Silver balls

1. Fill the wafer cone with sweets.
2. Coat the Marie biscuit with icing and place over the open end of the cone. Upend so that the biscuit forms the base.
3. Coat the cone with the icing and attach the lizard as illustrated.
4. Use the star nozzle to pipe a row of stars around the base of the cone.
5. Enhance with silver balls.

SHOO FLY!

Jelly (powder or cubes) – 5–6 servings per packet
125 ml clear plastic containers with lids
Self-adhesive silver stars
Plastic flies or bugs of choice
Clear plastic cocktail sticks
Prestik® or Blu-tac™
Green and silver curling ribbon

1. Make the jelly according to packet instructions, pour into the plastic containers and leave to set in the fridge.
2. Decorate the lid of the container with the stars.
3. Attach the fly to the blunt end of the cocktail stick with a blob of Prestik®.
4. Make a small slit in the centre of the lid with a sharp knife and insert the cocktail stick so that the fly hovers above the container.
5. Decorate with curling ribbon and place the lids on the containers before serving.

SWEET DREAMS

Wafer biscuits
Icing (page 160) – brown, green, yellow
Green edible glitter
White chocolate discs
Non-toxic food colouring pens – red, black
Toy beetles

1. Coat the top third of the biscuit with brown icing and use the star nozzle and green icing to create a sleeping bag. Sprinkle with edible glitter.
2. Place the chocolate disc on the brown icing, just touching the top edge of the green icing, to make the head.
3. Use the writing nozzle to ice spikes of yellow hair.
4. Draw the facial features as illustrated and place the toy beetle at the bottom edge of the sleeping bag.

CAMP SITE BIRTHDAY CAKE

1½ x Basic Cake (page 160) – one x cake baked in a 500 ml ovenproof bowl; one x 280 mm round cake
3 x wafer ice-cream cones
Icing (page 160) – light green, dark green, brown, blue, orange, red
200 g sugar paste
Powdered food colouring – red, brown
2 x peanut clusters, broken into smaller bits
Caramel crunch

Candy sticks
Green balls
Small piece of Flake® chocolate for the fire
A few red Astros™ or Skittles™ for the embers
1 x small male doll
Toy plastic snake, frog, lizard, monkey, spider and bats, or as preferred
Florist's wire, about 200 mm long

1. Prepare the cake batter as per the recipe. Pour the batter into the pudding bowl so that it fills to about three-quarter way, and then add the rest to the round tin. Bake until a skewer comes out clean when tested.

2. Trim sections from the base of two of the ice-cream cones, about 40 mm and 60 mm, so that the 'trees' are of differing heights. Use the star nozzle and a pull-out motion to cover the cones with light green icing. Set aside.

3. Use small pieces of white sugar paste to mould bases for the toadstools. Tint some more sugar paste with the red powdered food colouring and mould the tops of the toadstools. Add spots of white sugar paste.

4. Place the small cake flat side down and use icing to coat the top so that the contour is rounded.

5. Tint the remaining sugar paste with brown powdered food colouring and roll out to 2–4 mm thick on a surface that has been lightly dusted with icing sugar. Use to cover the small cake, trimming at the base to neaten.

6. Use a sharp knife to cut an arched doorway in the 'tent' and carefully remove a small section of the inside of the cake to create an entrance. Coat the inside of the entrance with brown icing.

7. Cover the top and sides of the large round cake with dark green icing and place the tent in position at the back of the cake, slightly off centre to the left. Use the star nozzle and brown icing to edge the doorway of the tent. Place the trees in position next to the tent.

8. Use a toothpick to mark off an area for a pathway and a stream. Fill in the stream with blue icing, roughening the surface slightly. Surround with pieces of the peanut clusters. Emphasize the lawn area with piped stars. Fill in the path with the caramel crunch and cut candy sticks into 20 mm lengths to create the fencing poles. Insert to line the pathway, topping each pole with a small dab of icing. Attach a large green ball to each pole.

9. Create a small fire on the lawn with the chocolate Flake® pieces and the Astros™. Spoon orange and red icing alongside each other into the icing tube and, using the star nozzle, pull out one or two flames.

10. Remove the legs from the doll, cover the base of the torso with a small piece of foil and place the doll in the tent entrance so that he peeps out from within.

11. Attach a toy plastic bat to one of the trees. Attach a spider or bat to the outside of the tent with a small blob of icing sugar. Arrange the plastic toy creatures on the cake to complement the camping scene.

FOR BREAKFAST THE FOLLOWING MORNING

Prepare a self-service spread of one or more of the following options: crumpets and waffles with a choice of syrup or jam and freshly whipped cream; mini muffins with a selection of jams; fresh fruit kebabs; a selection of mini boxed cereals with sugar and milk; assorted mini yoghurts. Include fresh fruit juice with all of these choices.

DOLLY'S

SETTING THE SCENE

This is a wonderful theme for your guests, who get to don their mums' finery and have their favourite baby doll accompany them to this special event!

❋ Tie white and yellow daisies with yellow and orange curling ribbon and attach to the front gate with yellow and orange balloons. Scatter petals or flowers from the gate to the front door. (Note: Should fresh flowers be unavailable, use artificial or tissue flowers throughout this theme.)

❋ Cover the table with yellow crepe paper and use a white lace or yellow tulle overlay. Arrange yellow and white daisies in teapots and place on the table and in the party area. Scatter petals and/or flowers on the floor around the party table. Create a canopy above the table by draping yellow and orange streamers from the centre of the ceiling to the edges. Tie yellow and orange balloons with curling ribbon and attach to the corners of the party area. Suspend yellow and orange ribbons from the ceiling and attach flowers and butterflies (available at craft shops) to the ends of the ribbons.

❋ Draw daisies on cardboard, paint with craft spray, decorate with glitter, cut out and attach to the walls in the party area. (Use the template on page 165 if preferred.)

❋ Set a place for each child with plastic teacups and saucers. Attach a large yellow tulle bow to the back of each chair. Write the guest's name on yellow board paper, decorate with glitter, punch a hole in one corner and attach to the bow with yellow curling ribbon. The children can take these home.

❋ Make placemats from cardboard using the daisy template (page 165). Colour with non-toxic craft paint.

❋ Cover a cardboard box with yellow crepe paper or paint with craft spray and decorate with flowers, ribbons, balloons and glitter. Fill with dressing-up clothes in case some of the children don't arrive in costume. You can also add accessories such as gloves, high-heeled shoes, hats and so on.

❋ Set aside a changing table for the dolls. Place small containers of baby talc (use under supervision) and baby lotion on the table. Be sure to include disposable baby doll diapers.

❋ Use all the doll accessories that you have and borrow extras from friends. These should include prams, beds, feeding chairs, clothes, and so on. Make another box in the same manner as the one described above, and use this for the dolls' clothes.

Recommended age group: 4–6

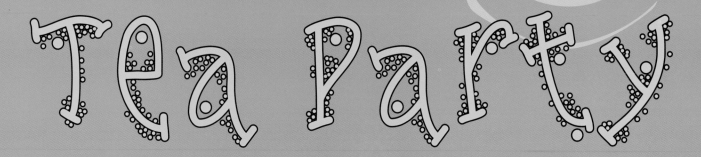

Tea Party

INVITATIONS

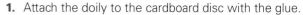

YOU WILL NEED (PER INVITATION):
1 x small gold paper doily
1 x cardboard disc, about 110 mm in diameter
Craft glue
1 x plastic doll's teacup and saucer
1 x small plastic spoon (optional)
Prestik® or Blu-tac™
Orange notepaper – 100 x 100 mm
Stapler
1 x 120 mm length of thin gold cord
Orange board paper nametag
Gold glitter glue

1. Attach the doily to the cardboard disc with the glue.
2. Place Prestik® on the bottom of the cup and press firmly to attach it to the saucer. Place another dab of Prestik® on the underside of the saucer and place on the doily, pressing firmly to secure. Attach a plastic spoon in the same manner if using.
3. Write the invitation details (see Suggested Wording) on the orange notepaper and fold up into a teabag shape (see page 165). Staple one end of the gold cord in place.
4. Write the guest's name on the nametag and decorate with glitter glue. Staple the free end of the teabag string to the nametag.
5. Place the teabag in the teacup and hand deliver!

SUGGESTED WORDING

Let's do tea to celebrate (child's name)'s birthday!
Meet at: the (child's surname) Tea Garden at (address)
Reservation from: (time party starts) to (time party ends)
RSVP: The head waitress at (phone number) by (date)
Dress: In your mum's finest!
Please bring your favourite baby doll

TREAT BAGS

YOU WILL NEED:
Teacup template (page 165)
Orange gift bags
Yellow board paper
Black felt-tip marker
Craft knife
Orange board paper nametags
Paper punch
120 mm lengths of thin gold cord
Adhesive tape
Craft glue
Flower motif/bead (optional)
Yellow and orange curling ribbon

1. Enlarge the teacup template to fit on the front of the bag and trace it onto the yellow board paper using the felt-tip marker. Cut out and complete by adding the inner lines. Cut a small slit in the inner area of the cup.
2. Write the guest's name on the orange board paper nametag, punch a hole in one corner and attach it to one end of the gold cord.
3. Insert the free end of the string through the slit in the teacup so that the nametag appears to hang over the edge of the cup. Secure with a piece of tape to the wrong side of the teacup.
4. Glue the cup to the front of the gift bag and attach a flower or bead motif, if using.
5. Tie yellow and orange curling ribbon around the handle to enhance.

GAMES AND ACTIVITIES

Apart from the following games, allow free time for playing with the dolls.

Arrange the Flowers

YOU WILL NEED (PER TEAM):

1 x large piece of cardboard with a drawing of a vase and stems protruding*

1 x felt-tip marker

Divide the children into two or more teams. Have the children stand in a line, one behind the other, and give the child in front a felt-tip marker.

On starter's orders, the child in front must run to the poster, draw a daisy at the end of one of the stems, then run back to the team and hand the pen to the next child in line. The game continues in the same manner until there is a winning team. The winners receive a prize, the rest receive tokens.

* One stem per team member.

Pass the Teapot

This game may be played at the table.

YOU WILL NEED:

1 x plastic teapot

Numbered pieces of paper (as per the number of guests)

Music

1 x basket containing numbered prizes (as per the number of guests)

Place the numbered paper squares in the teapot and have the children sit in a circle. Start the music and let the children pass the teapot from one to the other. When the music stops, the child who is holding the teapot chooses a number from the pot. She then picks a prize with the corresponding number from the basket. When a child has won a prize, she is eliminated from the game.

The music restarts and the game continues until all the children have received a prize.

Rock the Baby

YOU WILL NEED:

Music

Instruct the children to move about, rocking their babies to sleep in time to the music. When the music stops, they must stand still. The last child to stop moving is out. The game continues in this manner until there is a winner, who receives a prize. The rest receive tokens.

Pour the Tea

YOU WILL NEED (PER TEAM):

1 x plastic teacup with saucer

1 x plastic teapot

1 x empty bucket or similar container

1 x bucket filled with water (enough to pour a cup for each child in the team, and some more)

Appoint one child in each team to act as the pourer, and have the rest stand in a line behind the empty bucket at a predetermined distance from the pourer. The first child in line must hold an empty teacup and saucer.

On starter's orders, the pourer fills the teapot with water from the full bucket, while the first child runs toward her, balancing the teacup on the saucer.

The water must be poured into the teacup and the child must return to her team, trying not to spill. When she reaches her team, she must pour the water into the empty bucket before handing the cup and saucer to the next child in line, who then repeats the procedure.

The game continues until each child has had a turn and the water in each team's bucket is assessed to determine which contains the most water. The winning team receives a prize, the rest receive tokens.

PARTY FOOD

Cappuccino Cupcakes

Party Cupcakes (page 161)
Wafer cookie cups
Marie biscuits or Rich Tea™ biscuits
Icing (page 160) – brown, white
Round ring sweets
Cocoa powder
Gold balls
Pink balls

1. Bake the cupcakes in the wafer cookie cups as per the recipe. Cool completely.
2. Coat a Marie biscuit with brown icing, and then place a cupcake in the centre.
3. Cut the round sweet in half and attach one half to the side of the cookie cup with icing, to make the cup's ear.
4. Ice the cupcake with swirls of white icing, piling as high as possible to create a cappuccino-like topping. Dust with cocoa powder.
5. Place the gold and pink balls as illustrated to create a flower.

Dolly's Formula

Marie biscuits or Rich Tea™ biscuits
Icing (page 160) – orange, white
Tinkies® or Twinkies™
Silver balls
Orange marshmallow round
Dome-shaped sugared jelly sweets

1. Coat a Marie biscuit with orange icing.
2. Cover the Tinkie® with white icing and place upright on the biscuit.
3. Pipe a row of stars around the base to secure and place a silver ball on each star.
4. Attach the marshmallow sweet to the top of the 'bottle' and add the dome-shaped sweet to the centre of the marshmallow, securing with a small amount of icing.

Daisy Biscuits

Easy Biscuits (page 161)
Icing (page 160) – yellow
Flat milk chocolate rounds
Daisy cookie cutter or template (page 165)

1. Prepare the biscuit dough as per the recipe.
2. Use the cookie cutter to cut out the biscuits and bake as per the instructions. (If using the template, trace the shape onto cardboard and use to cut out the biscuits.)
3. Leave the biscuits to cool completely before covering with yellow icing.
4. Place the chocolate round in the centre of the flower.

My Favourite Dolly

Wafer biscuits
Icing (page 160) – orange, yellow, red
Marshmallow puff sweets
White chocolate discs
Candy sticks
Silver and blue balls

1. Coat the wafer biscuit with orange icing.
2. Cut the marshmallow sweet in half from the tip to the base and place one half cut side down on the biscuit.
3. Attach the chocolate disc for the head.
4. Cut the candy sticks into 20 mm lengths and place in position for the arms and legs, pushing gently into the icing to secure.
5. Decorate the doll's skirt with icing stars. Add an icing star at the neck and enhance with a silver ball.
6. Attach icing stars for shoes and place a silver ball on each.
7. Pipe the hair with yellow icing and add the facial features as illustrated, securing the eyes (blue balls) with a small dab of icing and using a writing nozzle to pipe on the mouth with red icing.

BABY DOLL BIRTHDAY CAKE

2½ x Basic Cake (page 160) –
   two x 300 x 240 mm cakes; one x 200 mm round cake
Icing (page 160) – yellow, orange, flesh-coloured
Mini Smarties®
Large gold balls
1 x plastic baby's dummy (pacifier)
2 x large googly eyes
Liquorice strips
1 x dome-shaped sugared jelly sweet
Caramel popcorn
1 x flat round sweet

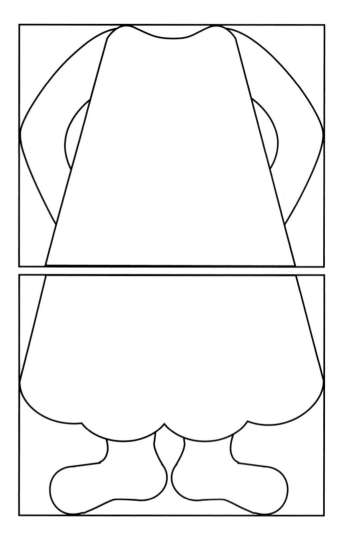

1. Bake the cakes as directed and leave
    to cool completely.
2. Cut out and assemble the cakes as per
    the cutting guides above. (Offcuts may be
    frozen and used at a later stage for a trifle.)
3. Position the round cake for the head.
4. Coat the sides and the top of the dress section
    with yellow icing, then use the star nozzle to
    decorate the entire dress with stars. Add
    orange edging as illustrated, as well as a collar.
5. Fashion flowers from the Smarties® and add
    gold balls to enhance the edging of the collar.
6. Pipe shoes and socks as illustrated, and attach
    a gold ball to each shoe.
7. Coat the arms and the head with the flesh-
    coloured icing.
8. Add a row of gold balls to one arm for a bangle.
9. Insert the dummy (pacifier) into the face and attach the googly eyes, adding small liquorice strips for eyelashes.
10. Cut the tip off the dome-shaped sweet and place the round section, cut side down, in position for the nose.
11. Add the popcorn hair and enhance with a Smarties® flower (coat the flat round sweet with icing to provide a firm
    base that will allow for easy placing in the popcorn, and attach the Smarties®).

SETTING THE SCENE

Don't be misled by the train – both girls and boys will have a hooting, tooting time aboard the Toyland Express!

- Combine bright colours for the décor – yellow, red, green, blue and purple.
- Attach a sign to the front gate with an arrow pointing to Toyland. Add a bunch of balloons tied together with trailing curling ribbon.
- Collect cardboard boxes of the same size, one for each child, and remove the top and bottom flaps. Cut holes in two opposite sides, large enough for the children to fit their arms through. To 'ride' about, the children will step into the box and keep it up around their bodies by fitting their arms through the slits. Spray or paint each box a different colour and attach streamers and decorations of choice. Attach a brightly coloured, helium-filled balloon to each box, arrange them one behind the other in a train fashion, and you are assured of a splendid display to greet the guests. Use bold lettering to write each guest's name on the box. (Guests may take these home at the end of the party.) Tape a coloured plastic whistle to each and allow 'passengers to board the train' with noisy enthusiasm as soon as the party gets underway.
- Cover the table with brightly coloured crepe paper. Attach matching twisted streamers to the centre of the ceiling above the party table and drape to the edges, securing with tape, to create a canopy.
- Attach strips of streamers to the edges of the ceiling so that they cascade down the walls. Intersperse with ropes of tinsel to add a sparkling effect.
- Attach curling ribbon to balloons and hang these at varying heights above the party table.
- Display toys of all descriptions throughout the party area as well as on the party table.
- The birthday mum may elect to be Toyland's fairy doll by wearing a pair of fairy wings with a fairy crown. Helpers may also enter into the spirit of the celebration by dressing up.

Recommended age group: 2-4

TRAVEL TO TOYLAND

INVITATIONS

Set up a family production line for these invitations!

YOU WILL NEED (PER INVITATION):

Train template (page 163)

Pencil

Thin cardboard measuring 180 x 120 mm

Scissors

Craft knife

±50 mm square piece of clear acetate

Adhesive tape

Selection of coloured paper

Craft glue

Notepaper

Glitter pen

Polyester fibre filling for the smoke

4 x glow-in-the-dark or self-adhesive stars

Silver glitter glue

1. Trace the outline of the template onto the cardboard and cut out.

2. Use the craft knife to remove the window section and tape the acetate in position on the underside of the train.

3. Refer to the photograph for use of colours and cut out the sections of the train using the template as a guide. Glue in position on the upper side of the train.

4. Write the invitation details (see Suggested Wording) on the notepaper and paste at the back of the train, taking care not to overlap into the acetate section.

5. Write the guest's name below the window using a glitter pen.

6. Glue the fibre filling to the chimney section to create the smoke and attach the stars to the wheels.

7. Dab a spot of glitter glue on the front of the engine and on the boiler behind the funnel and leave to dry.

SUGGESTED WORDING

All aboard (birthday child's name)'s Toyland Express!

Boarding from station at: (address) on (date)

Train departs at: (time party commences)

Journey ends at: (time party ends)

RSVP: The fairy doll at (phone number) by (date)

TREAT BAGS

YOU WILL NEED:

Party boxes

Small train motifs or stickers

Craft glue

Glitter pen

Curling ribbon – colours to match theme

Small magic springs

1. Assemble the party boxes and attach the train motifs with the glue (or use a sticker if preferred).
2. Write the guest's name on the side of the box with the glitter pen.
3. Tie the ribbons through the handle of the box and drape the magic spring as illustrated.

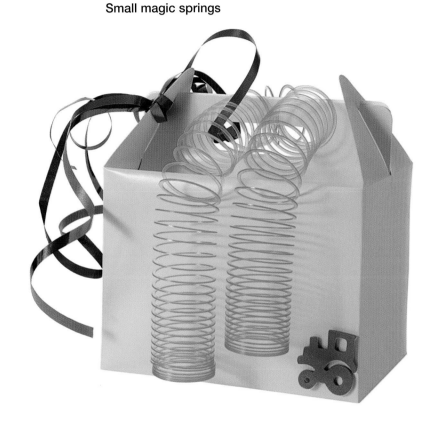

GAMES AND ACTIVITIES

Rather than organized games with prizes for this age group, allow free play with various stations set up where the tiny tots may amuse themselves as preferred.

Borrow extra toys from friends, or hire if necessary, to provide a sufficient variety to amuse the children. Encourage the children to board their 'train' by climbing into their respective boxes, and then to travel from station to station. Signpost the stations with large colourful posters, such as: Dolls' Docking Station; Musical Toys' Tracking; Whistling Wheels Station (this would be for tricycles, and so on); Animal Crossing (toy farm and wild animals); Ball Pond Siding; Building Blocks Bunker; Bouncing Balls Station; Mechanical Junction (wind-up toys); Puzzles Platform.

PARTY FOOD

SPINNING TOPS

Meringues (page 161)

Hundreds and thousands

Round marshmallow sweets

Icing (page 160) – colours per theme

Multicoloured dome-shaped sugared jelly sweets

1. Prepare the meringue mixture as per the recipe.
2. Trace 40 mm circles onto greaseproof paper and use to line a baking tray. Use a star nozzle to pipe swirls of meringe onto the circles, finishing with a point. Sprinkle with hundreds and thousands and bake as directed. Cool completely.
3. Attach the mallow sweet to the meringue with icing. Pipe a swirl of icing in the centre of the mallow sweet and insert the dome-shaped sweet.

MECHANICAL MICE

Sugar paste – pink

Party Cupcakes (page 161)

Icing (page 160) – white, pink

Marie biscuits or Rich Tea™ biscuits

Liquorice strips, cut into 80 mm lengths

Pink balls

Chocolate chips

Pink mini marshmallows

Chocolate bullets

1. Use a little sugar paste to mould the top of the key. Set aside to firm.
2. Bake the cupcakes as per the recipe. Cool completely. Trim the cupcakes into a mouse shape. Coat with white icing, shaping the front into a point.
3. Coat a Marie biscuit with pink icing and attach the cupcake. Use a wooden skewer to make a small hole at the tail end of the cupcake. Dip one end of the liquorice into icing and push it into the hole for the tail. Fill the surround with icing. Curve the tail.
4. Use pink balls for the eyes and a chocolate chip for the nose. Use slices of mini marshmallow for ears.
5. Insert the chocolate bullet into the back of the mouse and attach the top of the key with icing.

KOOKY KITES

Easy Biscuits (page 161)

Kite template (page 163)

Icing (page 160) – use two colours as per theme

Liquorice strips

Small star-shaped sweets

Silver balls

Liquorice Allsorts Mini™ sweets

1. Prepare the biscuit dough according to the recipe.
2. Use the template to cut out the biscuits and bake as directed. Leave to cool completely.
3. Coat the biscuit with icing and decorate with the liquorice strips as illustrated. Attach stars and balls.
4. Separate the layers of the Liquorice Allsorts Mini™ sweets, cut out bows and attach to the tail at intervals, securing each with icing.

JACK-IN-THE-BOXES

Wafer biscuits

Icing (page 160) – colours as per theme, plus red

Small star-shaped sweets

Apricot half sweets

Round apricot sweets

Sugared jelly ring sweets

Dome-shaped sugared jelly sweets

Silver balls

1. Halve the biscuits across the width. Sandwich three halves on top of each other with icing for the box. Coat with icing and add star sweets as illustrated.
2. Place an apricot half sweet, flat side down, on top of the box. Top with a second sweet, securing with icing.
3. Use icing to attach the round apricot sweet head. Place in the fridge for 30 minutes to firm the icing.
4. Halve the ring sweets and attach with icing to make the arms. Use a dome-shaped sweet for the hat.
5. Pipe stars around the rim of the hat and on the tip. Pipe a ruff around the neck. Add silver balls.
6. Attach silver balls for the eyes and use the writing nozzle to pipe a red smiley mouth.

TOYLAND EXPRESS CAKE

1 x Basic Cake (page 160) – 300 x 240 mm
Icing (page 160) – yellow, purple, flesh-coloured, green, red
1 x small toy doll
Disposable see-through food container, about 110 mm wide, trimmed to size to fit cab
1 x ready-made swiss roll – 180 x 90 mm
2 x googly eyes
1 x small dome-shaped sugared jelly sweet

1 x mouth-shaped sweet
Large and small silver balls
1 x long, straight, multi-coloured lollipop
1 x small tuft of polyester fibre filling
10 x apricot half sweets
8 x orange round marshmallow sweets
Candy sticks
Smarties®, Jelly Beans™ or other sweets of choice

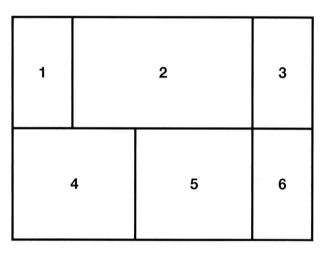

1 = Front wedge
2 = Base for swiss roll
3 = Cab
4 = Truck 1
5 = Truck 2
6 = Upper cab

1. Bake the cake as per the recipe and leave to cool completely before cutting out as per the guide above.

2. Trim one end of the base section into a wedge shape by slicing through with a sharp knife.

3. Place the upper cab section on the opposite end of the base section, sandwiching together with a layer of icing. Coat the base and the cab with yellow icing.

4. Remove the legs from the doll and insert the torso into the cake. Place the plastic container on the cab, gently pressing in so that it covers the doll. (You may need to support the centre back section of the container with a wooden skewer inside of a plastic straw and inserted into the cake.) Pipe small yellow stars lightly around the base of the window section and along the top and outer edges as illustrated.

5. Cut the swiss roll to size if necessary, place on top of the base and coat along the length with purple icing.

6. Cover the face end with the flesh-coloured icing. Place the googly eyes in position on the face. Place the dome-shaped sugared jelly sweet in position for the nose and attach the mouth-shaped sweet. Pipe a row of stars around the face to neaten the outline and pipe stars as illustrated along the edges of the swiss roll.

7. Pipe stars on the cowcatcher as illustrated and enhance with silver balls. Gently insert the lollipop into the swiss roll and attach a tuft of fibre filling for the smoke. Place two apricot half sweets, flat side down, on top of the swiss roll and pipe stars as illustrated, topping each star with a large silver ball.

8. Place the orange mallow sweets in position along each side of the engine. Pipe a star in the centre of each wheel and attach a large silver ball.

9. Hollow out a section in the centre top of each truck before coating the entire truck with icing, one green and one red. Link the trucks to the engine with the candy sticks. Attach the apricot half sweets for the wheels and decorate with a star and a large silver ball, as for the engine. Place the sweets in the trucks.

Bling Bling

SETTING THE SCENE

Creative talent will be unleashed and bling will be the order of the day as bowls of beads evolve into awe-inspiring jewellery! Guests will be delighted to accessorize their favourite outfits with their precious pieces!

* All the guests will need to be seated around a central work station, so ensure that you have sufficient space before determining the number of guests to be invited.
* Use iridescent or pearlised balloons in pale pastel colours of choice throughout this theme.
* Tie a bunch of balloons together with curling ribbon and attach to the front gate. Lay a trail of florist's gemstones from the front gate to the party area. Suspend a beaded curtain in the front doorway.
* Prepare two tables, one as the party table with eats, and the second as the work station. Cover the party table with strips of pastel crepe paper. Arrange garlands of beads and other jewellery on the table.
* Use twisted strips of pastel crepe paper to create a canopy above the party table. Suspend the strips from the centre of the ceiling to the edges. Attach bundles of pastel-coloured balloons to the corners of the ceiling. Colour polystyrene balls with non-toxic craft paint and use a screwdriver or firm piece of wire to make a hole through the centre of each ball. Thread fishing line through the balls to string them together. Drape the strings of balls along the walls of the party area.
* Attach fishing line to individual balls and suspend them above the party table at varying heights.
* Cover the work station with a suitable tablecloth and create a place setting for each guest – use a small hand towel for each setting to prevent the beads rolling away.
* At each setting, place small transparent plastic bowls containing beads, clasps and other materials.
* Use a jewellery lady, draped with strings of beads, as a centrepiece on this table.
* Place small bowls of sweets and popcorn on this table so that guests may have something to nibble on while they work.
* Provide soft background music to complement the scene and enhance the craft work experience.

Recommended age group: 7–12

Beads

INVITATIONS

YOU WILL NEED (PER INVITATION):
Pastel board paper for invitation details,
± 100 mm square (colour of choice)
Glitter pen
Paper punch
Pastel board paper for nametag
(colour to match above)
Silver cord, about 120 mm long
Prestik® or Blu-tac™
Elastic cord – up to 250 mm long
(170–180 mm is used for the beads,
the excess allows for ease of handling)
Beads of choice
One crimp for beading

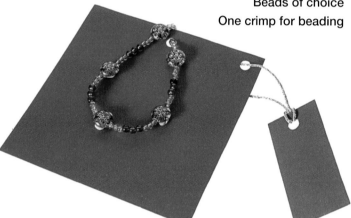

1. Write the invitation details (see Suggested Wording) on one side of the board paper using the glitter pen. Punch a hole near one corner.
2. Write the guest's name on the nametag with the glitter pen, punch a hole near the edge and attach to the invitation with the silver cord. Punch another hole in the centre top edge of the invitation.
3. Place a blob of Prestik® over one end of the elastic cord to prevent the beads falling off, then thread beads onto 170–180 mm of the cord.
4. Pass one end of the elastic cord through the central hole in the invitation so that the bracelet will be attached to the card.
5. Hold the two end points together and thread both through the crimp. Slide the crimp along the cord to touch the beads and squash firmly to secure. Cut off the excess cord.

SUGGESTED WORDING
Please BEAD at (child's name)'s birthday party on (date)
Gem store: (address)
Doors open: (time party starts)
Store closes: (time party ends)
RSVP: The Jeweller at (phone number) before (date)

TREAT BAGS

The guests will be so happy to take their jewellery home in these!

YOU WILL NEED (PER BAG):
Organza fabric (colour of choice) –
400 x 200 mm
Needle and thread
Length of cord or ribbon
(same colour as the fabric),
about 850 mm long
2 x large beads
1 x fabric flower
Board paper for nametag
(same colour as fabric)
Glitter pen

1. Fold the material in half and sew together along the two side edges. Leave the top open for the cord.
2. Turn down about 15 mm and hem to form a casing. Leave about 15 mm free on each side to insert the cord or ribbon.
3. Thread the cord through the casing. Match up the ends on each side; thread a bead onto the cord and knot around the bead to secure.
4. Stitch the fabric flower to the front of the bag.
5. Write the guest's name on the nametag and place the tag inside the bag.

GAMES AND ACTIVITIES

No games are necessary. Prepare the activity materials prior to the start of the party.

Necklace

YOU WILL NEED (PER NECKLACE):
2 x crimps
1 x 500 mm length fishing line
   (cut 40 mm or 50 mm extra and then trim later)*
Clasp
Small craft pliers

To be prepared in advance of the party: Thread a crimp onto one end of the fishing line then add one half of the clasp. Take the end of the fishing line and thread it back through the crimp and squash with the pliers.

At the party, have the children thread their beads onto the fishing line. To finish off, attach a crimp and the second half of the clasp. Twist the end of the thread back through the crimp and squash with pliers to secure.

If the children are creating a particular pattern or adding certain feature beads, it is easier for them if you mark the midpoint of the fishing line with a felt-tip marker. Successive marks could be made depending on the design that they are using.

Ring

Select a suitable adornment for the ring and secure in position with craft glue. Set aside to dry.

Bracelet

YOU WILL NEED (PER BRACELET):
1 x 180 mm length fishing line
   (cut 40 mm or 50 mm extra and then trim later)*
2 x crimps
Clasp
Small craft pliers

Follow the same instructions as for the necklace.

* Elastic cord is an alternative option – thread the beads onto the cord, then pass each of the two ends through a crimp and squash to secure.

Straight Pin

Select a few suitable beads or preferred adornment, and use craft glue to attach to the pin. Set aside to dry.

PARTY FOOD

Please BEAD Mine!

Easy Biscuits (page 161)
Ring template (page 165)
Icing (page 160) – white, pink
Pink edible glitter

1. Prepare the biscuit dough as per the recipe and use the template to cut out the biscuits.
2. Bake as directed and leave to cool completely.
3. Coat the ring band with white icing and use the star nozzle to decorate the jewel section with pink icing.
4. Sprinkle the jewel with edible glitter.

Jewellery Ladies

Use icing, lollipops and pipe cleaners of various colours for these appealing additions to your table décor.

Marie biscuits or Rich Tea™ biscuits
Icing (page 160) – green
Small sweets of choice
Wafer ice-cream cones
Pipe cleaners, 120 mm in length
Large green balls
Plastic rings
Lollipops
Candy necklaces

1. Coat the top of a Marie biscuit with icing.
2. Place a few small sweets in the cone, cover the cone with the biscuit and upend so that the biscuit forms the base. Use the star nozzle to pipe stars around the base of the cone.
3. Gently insert the pipe cleaner through the cone from one side to the other. Curl the ends by twisting them around a wooden skewer.
4. Pipe stars down the centre front of the cone and place a large shiny green ball on each.
5. Slip a ring over the tip of the cone and gently insert the stick of the lollipop into the tip of the cone so that just the round part of the lollipop protrudes.
6. Drape a candy necklace over the pipe cleaner.

A Lucky Locket

Marie biscuits or Rich Tea™ biscuits
Icing (page 160) – white
White edible glitter
Small oval-shaped sweets
Heart-shaped sweets

1. Sandwich two biscuits together with icing. Coat the upper biscuit with a layer of icing and sprinkle with edible glitter.
2. Arrange the oval sweets in the shape of a necklace, with the heart positioned in the centre at the bottom.

A Gem of a Treat

Strings of beads
Plastic parfait glasses
Plastic spoons
Prestik®, Blu-tac™ or other adhesive
Ice cream
Lollipops

1. Loop the beads around the base of the glass and attach the opposite end to the under edge of the spoon handle using a small dab of adhesive material to secure.
2. Place a generous scoop of ice cream into the glass.
3. Position the spoon in the ice cream so that the beads cascade down the side of the glass.
4. Insert a lollipop into the top of the ice cream.

BIRTHDAY BEADS CAKE

1½ x Basic Cake (page 160), baked in ovenproof pudding bowls of the following capacities:
   1 x 1 500 ml; 2 x 500 ml; 2 x 250 ml; 2 x 75 ml; 6 x 50 ml
Icing (page 160) – turquoise, yellow, lilac, lime green, pink
250 g sugar paste
Yellow powdered food colouring
Large silver balls
1 x 300 mm-long silver pipe cleaner

1. Divide the cake mixture between the bowls and bake at 180 °C (350 °F, Gas Mark 4), taking special note that the smallest cakes will cook in about 15 minutes, whereas the largest cake will take 45–60 minutes because of the depth. Test the remaining cakes at intervals, inserting a wooden skewer to assess whether they are done.
2. Leave all the cakes to cool completely. Use a serrated knife to trim the top of the cakes if necessary for a flat surface and to ensure that matching sizes are equal in depth.
3. Coat the six small (50 ml) cakes with a thin layer of icing, rounding the contour so that when placed flat-side down they will resemble beads.
4. Colour the sugar paste yellow and roll out to 2–4 mm thick. Use to cover the small cakes.
5. Position the remaining cakes flat-side down and coat with a thin layer of icing, rounding the contours before using the star nozzle to decorate as illustrated, or as preferred.
6. Place the smaller cakes in between to link the 'beads' together.
7. Enhance the beads with silver balls.
8. Twist the pipe cleaner around a pencil to curl, cut in half and insert one half into each of the end beads for the cord.

Wintry

SETTING THE SCENE

*Brighten up a winter birthday with these fun ideas,
or use as a refreshingly white party in the heat of summer!*

* Tie a bunch of white and silver balloons together with white and silver curling ribbon and attach to the front gate. Lay a trail of white polystyrene chips from the front gate to the party entrance.

* Cut out a snowman from cardboard and use non-toxic craft spray to decorate. Add a hat and eyes. Attach a carrot for the nose and tie a scarf around the neck. Stand it on a bed of white polyester fibre filling that has been dusted with silver glitter. Place at the front entrance to welcome the guests.

* Wind white streamers around garden shrubs and pot plants and attach small bundles of fibre filling to resemble freshly fallen snow. Sprinkle silver glitter over the fibre filling.

* Thread cotton balls onto lengths of fishing line and suspend in the doorway to represent falling snow. Spread white sheets on the floor and cover with white balloons for the children to wade through.

* Cover the table with white crepe paper and top with bunched white tulle fabric. Sprinkle with silver confetti. Decorate the table with snowman figurines, polar bears and other winter ornaments. Create a white canopy of streamers above the table by draping them from the centre of the ceiling to the edges. Suspend white streamers vertically down the walls, interspersed with silver tinsel.

* Paint polystyrene balls of varying sizes and dust lightly with silver glitter. Attach fishing line and suspend above the table at varying heights. Intersperse with white and silver doilies to emulate snowflakes.

* Make cardboard cutouts of snowmen and attach to the walls of the party area.

* Attach white and silver doilies to the windows. Use snow spray on as many surfaces as possible.

* Create a blizzard! As guests arrive, hand them a packet of white confetti, which they may use to sprinkle on guests. Be prepared for a mess and a great deal of fun, as children love the magic of confetti.

Recommended age group: 6–12

Wishes

INVITATIONS

Allow plenty of time to make these invitations and enlist the assistance of the entire family, as an 'assembly line' will speed up the process. The end result will delight the recipients and set the tone for a successful party. For a simpler option, if preferred, enlarge the template used for the treat bag, write the invitation details on the back and decorate.

YOU WILL NEED (PER INVITATION):

White notepaper – cut to the same size as the cake board

1 x mini silver cake board or a stiff cardboard disc painted with silver non-toxic craft spray – about 100 mm in diameter

Craft glue

2 x polystyrene balls – 50 mm and 40 mm in diameter

Scissors

1 x strip thin cardboard (type that is used for the inners of gift wrap) – 110 x 20 mm

2 x stiff cardboard circles – 25 mm and 40 mm in diameter

Black non-toxic craft spray

Scraps of orange and red felt

2 x googly eyes

Silver ribbon – 200 mm long

2 x red beads

1 x 300 mm-long silver pipe cleaner

Polyester fibre filling

Silver glitter

1 x white board paper circle – 35 mm in diameter

Silver glitter glue

Paper punch

Thin silver cord

1. Write the invitation details (see Suggested Wording) on the notepaper. Glue underneath the cake board.
2. Assemble the snowman by gluing the larger polystyrene ball to the cake board and then attaching the smaller ball for the head.
3. Wind the thin cardboard strip around your finger to fashion the body of the hat, adjust to fit the 25 mm stiff cardboard circle and glue the ends. Attach the tube to the smaller circle using craft glue. Coat the central section of the 40 mm circle with glue and attach the open end of the tube to this. Leave to dry and then paint the hat black. Set aside to dry.
4. Cut a nose and mouth from the felt and glue these in place, along with the googly eyes.
5. Wind the ribbon around the neck, trimming the ends and securing with glue.
6. Attach the bead buttons with craft glue.
7. To make the arms, cut two 50 mm lengths and two 40 mm lengths from the pipe cleaner. Wind one shorter length around one end of the 50 mm piece to resemble fingers. Repeat for the second arm. Insert the arms into either side of the body.
8. Draw a line of glue around the base of the snowman and attach the fibre filling. Sprinkle lightly with glitter.
9. Write the guest's name on the back of the white board paper, and decorate the front with glitter glue. Punch a hole near the edge, feed the cord through the hole and knot the ends together. Hang the nametag over an arm.

SUGGESTED WORDING

Frolic with snowmen at (child's name)'s birthday party.

Winter wonderland: (party address)

Snow will blanket activities on: (date) at (time party starts)

Snow will melt at: (time party ends)

RSVP: Frosty the Snowman at (phone number) before (date)

Dress: White!

TREAT BAGS

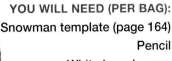

YOU WILL NEED (PER BAG):
Snowman template (page 164)
Pencil
White board paper
Scissors
Black felt-tip marker
2 x googly eyes
4 x silver beads
Craft glue
Red felt or felt-tip marker
1 x small silver bow
Silver glitter glue
1 x silver gift bag
Polyester fibre filling
for snow
Silver glitter
Paper punch
Silver curling ribbon

1. Enlarge the template and trace it onto the white board paper. Cut out and colour the hat section with the felt-tip marker.
2. Attach the googly eyes and glue on a bead for the nose. Cut out a mouth from the felt and glue in place or draw in a mouth with the felt-tip marker.
3. Glue the bow in position and attach three beads to the upper body for the buttons. Decorate the lower body with glitter glue.
4. Coat the back of the snowman with glue and attach to the front of the bag. Attach fibre filling to the bag to resemble snow and dust lightly with glitter.
5. Cut a 40 mm-diameter circle from board paper, decorate with glitter glue and set aside to dry. Write the guest's name on the back of the circle.
6. Punch a hole near the edge of the nametag and attach to the handle of the bag with curling ribbon.

GAMES AND ACTIVITIES

Build a Snowman

Provide materials similar to those required for the invitation. Set aside a work station to accommodate the guests, cover with white crepe paper and top with a layer of clear plastic. Place the materials in containers along the centre of the table so that they are within easy reach. Egg boxes are excellent containers for beads, googly eyes and other small bits. Assemble the hats (refer to the invitation details) prior to the party and enlist the help of a friend to assist the children if necessary.

Hold a snowman parade when they have all been assembled and award small prizes, ensuring that there is one for each snowman.

Under Winter Wraps

YOU WILL NEED (PER GROUP):
One or more toilet rolls
1 x suitable hat
1 x winter scarf
Other props as preferred

Divide the children into groups of four or five. Each group must choose a candidate to be the snowman.

On starter's orders, the remaining members of the team must wrap their snowman in toilet paper – faces must be kept open. After the snowman is wrapped, finish off with the hat and scarf and other props. The first group to finish receives a prize, the rest receive tokens.

PARTY FOOD

Wintry Waddles

Small sweets of choice
Wafer cookie cups
Marie biscuits or Rich Tea™ biscuits
Icing (page 160) – white
White edible glitter
Silver balls
Penguin-shaped sweets

1. Place the sweets in the cookie cup.
2. Coat the Marie biscuit with icing and use to cover the cookie cup. Upend so that the biscuit forms the base.
3. Coat the cookie cup with icing and use the star nozzle to pipe stars around the base and along the upper edge.
4. Dust with edible glitter and enhance the upper layer of stars with silver balls.
5. Place the penguin sweet in position on the top of the cookie cup, pressing gently to secure.

Sweet Slalom

Wafer biscuits
Icing (page 160) – white
White edible glitter
Liquorice straps
Lollipop sticks
Small dolls
Mini Smarties® – two per treat

1. Coat the wafer biscuit with icing and sprinkle with edible glitter.
2. Cut the liquorice straps into narrow strips to fit the length of the wafer biscuit and shape the front ends into points. Place two strips (skis) onto the biscuits, parallel to each other, pressing gently to secure.
3. Cut the lollipop sticks to fit the doll and attach to the hands with icing or a small dab of Prestik®.
4. Attach the doll to the skis with a dab of icing and place mini Smarties® at each end of the ski pole.

Wintry Berry Bush

Party Cupcakes (page 161)
Marie biscuits or Rich Tea™ biscuits
Icing (page 160) – white
Red Mini Astros™ or Skittles™
White edible glitter

1. Bake the cupcakes as per the recipe. Leave to cool.
2. Trim the cupcakes so that the tops are level.
3. Coat the Marie biscuit with icing and place the cupcake upside down on the Marie biscuit.
4. Use the star nozzle and a pull-out motion to cover the cupcake with 'branches'.
5. Add Mini Astros™ as illustrated and sprinkle the cupcake with edible glitter.

Frosty Snowmen

Sugar paste – white
Marie biscuits or Rich Tea™ biscuits
Icing (page 160) – white, orange
Sweetie Pies® or Tunnock's Tea Cakes™
Silver curling ribbon – about 100 mm for each treat
Rolo® chocolates
Milk chocolate discs
Large and small silver balls
Blue balls for the eyes
Red non-toxic food colouring pen

1. Roll a walnut-sized ball of sugar paste for each treat. Set aside to firm. This will be the head.
2. Coat the top of a Marie biscuit with white icing and attach the Sweetie Pie® so that the biscuit forms the base. Cover the Sweetie Pie® with white icing.
3. Twist the curling ribbon on top so that it forms a scarf, wedging it in slightly. Place the head in position, adding extra icing if necessary to secure.
4. For the hat, attach the Rolo® to the chocolate disc with icing. Place on the head. Attach the silver balls.
5. Attach the blue balls for eyes and use the writing nozzle and orange icing to 'tweak' out a nose.
6. Draw the mouth with the colouring pen.
7. Affix the large silver balls for the buttons.

THE SWEETEST SNOWMAN CAKE

2 x Basic Cake (page 160) – each baked in 1 x 1.5 litre ovenproof pudding bowl and 1 x 0.5 litre pudding bowl,
   thus providing 2 of each. Also 1 x small (about 400 g) food can.
Icing (page 160) – white, black, orange
Wooden skewers
Firm cardboard circle – 120 mm diameter
Large and small silver balls
2 x googly eyes
1 x wafer ice-cream cone
7 x small round red sweets
3 x round orange sweets
Silver ribbon – 600 mm long
2 x 300 mm-long silver pipe cleaners
2 x 8 mm-diameter dowel sticks – 150 mm long, covered with foil
White edible glitter

1. Prepare the cake batter. Grease and line the small food can and half fill with batter – this is for the hat. Divide
    the rest of the batter between two x 1.5 litre and two x 0.5 litre ovenproof pudding bowls. Bake the cakes
    (the 1.5 litre cakes must be baked for 50–60 minutes) and leave to cool completely.
2. Use a serrated knife to level all surfaces. Place one large cake on a cake board with the flat side up, coat with
    a layer of white icing and attach the matching half to form the body of the snowman.
3. Place a smaller cake, flat side up, on top of the body, coat the surface with white icing and attach the matching
    half to form the head. Insert wooden skewers to secure the head to the body.
4. Coat the whole snowman with white icing, roughening the surface with the tip of a knife.
5. Cut a small hole in the centre of the cardboard circle (for the brim of the hat) and coat the upper side with
    black icing.
6. Attach the small cylindrical-shaped cake to the brim of the hat and coat the sides with black icing.
7. Insert a wooden skewer into the centre top of the hat, through the hole in the brim and attach the hat to the
    snowman's head, pressing the skewer into the snowman to secure. Coat the top of the hat with black icing
    and decorate the brim with large silver balls.
8. Attach the googly eyes to the face.
9. Trim about 30 mm from the tip of the wafer cone and discard the rest. Coat the cone tip with orange icing and
    press into the face (for the nose), ensuring that it is embedded.
10. Place the small red sweets in position for the smiling mouth.
11. Press the flat orange sweets into the body for buttons and surround each with small silver balls.
12. Wind the ribbon around the neck and overlap to one side so that it resembles a scarf. Neaten the ends with
    pinking shears and press into the icing to secure.
13. Cut a 120 mm length of pipe cleaner and twist around the dowel stick to form the outer fingers. Cut a 60 mm
    length of pipe cleaner and bend one end to hook into the back of the pipe cleaner loop on the dowel stick.
    Add a dab of Prestik® to secure. Repeat the procedure for the second dowel stick.
14. Insert the dowel sticks into the body on either side, at a slight angle, to form the arms.
15. Dust the smiling snowman with a light sprinkling of edible glitter.

Chocolate

SETTING THE SCENE

Wall-to-wall chocolate ... with more to take home!

* Wrap a large rectangle of polystyrene foam in gold foil and then cover with a strip of brown paper, to resemble a huge chocolate bar. Write the birthday child's name with gold glitter glue and attach to the front gate. Decorate with balloons in shades of brown and gold, and gold curling ribbon.

* Coat cardboard discs (diameter about 20 cm) in shades of brown and gold craft paint. Lay a trail from the front gate to the entrance. Smother garden shrubs and pot plants with strands of 'chocolate' by using crepe paper streamers in shades of brown. Hang giant chocolates (see below) on the branches.

* Thread wrapped chocolate sweets on lengths of fishing line and suspend in the doorway to create a chocolate curtain. Intersperse with non-chocolate, wrapped sweets if preferred. These may be taken down at the end of the party and distributed to the children to add to their treat bags.

* Make wrapped chocolate decorations to attach to the walls in the party area:
  – Cover polystyrene balls with pieces of coloured cellophane that are large enough to cover the ball and have sufficient on either side to twist like a sweet wrapper. Tie each twist with gold curling ribbon.
  – Cover polystyrene squares with gold foil and attach coloured paper shapes to the centre of each.

* Lay chocolate brown sheets on the floor of the party area or use shredded crepe paper to create a sea of chocolate. Cover with brown balloons so that the children may wade through a sea of chocolate.

* Cover the party table with chocolate brown crepe paper and top with a piece of gold organza fabric, bunched in places. Place small polystyrene balls, covered as described above, randomly on the table. Sprinkle gold confetti, gold ribbon curls and mini chocolate bars on the table.

* Create a canopy over the table with twisted streamers in shades of brown draped from the centre of the ceiling to the outer edges. Tie balloons in shades of brown and gold in the corners of the room. Cascade streamers in shades of brown vertically down the walls. Intersperse with gold tinsel ropes.

* Thread wrapped sweets and chocolates at intervals onto fishing line and suspend over the party table.

Recommended age group: 6–12

Factory

INVITATIONS

YOU WILL NEED:
Notepaper
Gold curling ribbon
Small clear plastic containers
Gold foil-wrapped chocolates
Gold discs for nametags
Felt-tip marker
Paper punch

1. Write the invitation details (see Suggested Wording) on the notepaper, fold to fit inside the container and tie with ribbon. Place in the container.
2. Add about four chocolates to the container and cover with the lid.
3. Tie the curling ribbon around the container.
4. Write the guest's name on the gold disc with the felt-tip marker. Punch a hole near the edge; thread the ribbon tied around the container through the hole and knot to secure.

SUGGESTED WORDING
Chocolate will flow at (child's name)'s birthday party.
Melt it, Mould it and Make it on: (date)
The Chocolate Factory: (address)
Production shift starts at: (time party starts)
Production shift ends at: (time party ends)
RSVP: Production Foreman at (phone number) by (date)
Dress: Brown!

TREAT BAGS

YOU WILL NEED:
Gold paper doilies
Gold disposable party plates
Prestik® or Blu-tac™
Disposable cake domes to fit the plates
Gold curling ribbon
Self-adhesive gold gift bows
Chocolate brown stiff card for the nametags
Gold glitter pen
Paper punch

1. Place the doily on the plate, securing with a small blob of Prestik®, and cover with the dome.
2. Place the ribbons on the self-adhesive strip of the gift bow and attach the bow to the centre of the cake dome.
3. Write the guest's name on the nametag with the glitter pen and punch a hole near one side edge. Thread curling ribbon through the hole and knot to secure.
4. Attach the nametag to the cake dome by tying it around the gift bow.

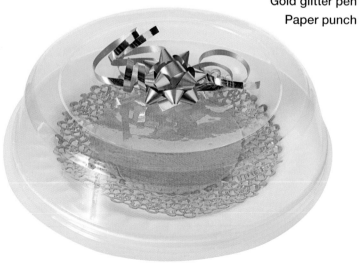

GAMES AND ACTIVITIES

The chocolate production will keep the children busy for most of the party, so no games are necessary.

Activity 1: Chocolate Making

YOU WILL NEED:

1 x table covered with brown crepe paper and topped with plastic

Selection of chocolate moulds – fairly small in size with a shallow form to allow for quick setting

Selection of chocolate – milk, white, mint flavoured, nutty, and other flavours of choice

Teaspoons – one per guest

Small cellophane packets – one per guest

Coloured curling ribbon

Stickers or self-adhesive stars

Set up the production table where the children may make their own chocolates. Enlist the help of one or two friends to melt the chocolate as per the manufacturer's instructions and use small containers for easy distribution among the children.

Let the children select their moulds and have felt-tip markers on hand to mark sections on the moulds with their names if they are sharing. Place the bowls of melted chocolate down the centre of the table and leave children to make their choices. They may use a teaspoon to scoop and pour the chocolate. Once they have filled the moulds, tap gently on the table to remove bubbles and place in the freezer until set (minimum 10–15 minutes, depending on the size of the mould).

When the children have completed this activity have them move on to Activity 2 until their chocolates have set. Clear the equipment from the table and replace with small cellophane packets and strips of coloured curling ribbon. Provide stickers and/or adhesive stars with which to decorate the packets.

When the chocolates have set, the children should once again congregate at this table to unmould their chocolates and put them into the cellophane packets. The packets are tied with the ribbon to secure. These make ideal take-home gifts! If preferred, they may pack their chocolates straight into their treat bags.

Activity 2: Ice-cream Parlour

YOU WILL NEED:

1 x table covered with brown crepe paper and topped with plastic

Plastic parfait glasses – one per guest

Plastic spoons – one per guest

Selection of ice creams

Ice-cream scoops

Selection of toppings – Melted chocolate, of course, as well as cherries, mini sweets and marshmallows, coloured sprinkles, nuts, mini chocolate flakes, wafer biscuits, and chocolate, caramel and strawberry syrups

Set up the second production table in the same manner as the first. Place a plastic parfait glass and a plastic spoon at each setting. Position suitable container/s filled with ice blocks on which you may place the tubs of ice cream in the centre of the table. You may prefer to have this on a separate table adjacent to the 'assembly line'. Your helpers will ensure that the ice cream isn't allowed to melt, and will return the containers to the freezer when necessary.

Place the selection of toppings in small containers within easy reach of the children so that they may help themselves (provide assistance if required).

Provide popular background music throughout the duration of these activities.

PARTY FOOD

The House of Chocolate

Marie biscuits or Rich Tea™ biscuits

Icing (page 160) – light brown, chocolate

Wafer biscuits

Chocolate vermicelli

Chocolate bullets

Liquorice Allsorts Mini™ sweets, separated
  into layers

Gold balls

Chocolate chips

1. Coat the top of a Marie biscuit with light brown icing.
2. Cut a wafer biscuit in half across the width and shape one edge of each half to resemble a roof.
3. Sandwich the two halves together with chocolate icing and place upright on the biscuit as shown.
4. Cover the house in chocolate icing and coat the roof with vermicelli.
5. Cut the chocolate bullet in half at a 45-degree angle and place one half on the roof for a chimney.
6. Position the Liquorice Allsorts Mini™ layers for windows and a door. Attach a gold ball with a dab of icing to make a doorknob.
7. Lay a path to the front door with the chocolate chips.

Decadent Butterflies

Party Cupcakes (page 161)

Gold foil cookie cups (baking cases)

Icing (page 160) – chocolate

Chocolate discs encrusted with hundreds
  and thousands

Large gold balls

Small gold balls

1. Bake the cupcakes in the cookie cups according to the recipe and leave to cool completely.
2. Coat the cupcake with chocolate icing and place two chocolate discs at an angle on the top of the cake, to resemble the butterfly's wings.
3. Use one large gold ball for the head and four small gold balls to make up the body.

Chocolate Gifts

To add to the fun, you may place a small numbered piece of folded paper under the disc. Guests may choose a corresponding numbered gift from a basket.

Easy Biscuits (page 161)

Melted baking chocolate

White chocolate discs

Icing (page 160) – white

Gold curling ribbon

1. Prepare the biscuit dough as per the recipe and cut into 70 x 40 mm rectangles.
2. Bake as directed and leave to cool completely.
3. Coat the biscuits with the melted chocolate and leave to set.
4. Attach the white chocolate disc with a small dab of icing and tie the ribbon around the chocolate bar.

Chocolate Blossoms

Wafer cookie cups

Small sweets of choice

Marie biscuits or Rich Tea™ biscuits

Icing (page 160) – chocolate

Milk chocolate discs

Round white chocolates

Silver edible glitter

1. Place the small sweets in the cookie cup.
2. Coat the Marie biscuit with icing and place over the open end of the cookie cup. Upend so that the biscuit forms the base.
3. Coat the flat top of the cookie cup with icing and place four chocolate discs in position for the petals.
4. Attach the round white chocolate to the centre, fixing with a small dab of icing.
5. Dust the petals with a light coating of edible glitter.

CHOCOLATE MILL CAKE

2 x Basic Cake (page 160) – two x 300 x 240 mm cakes
Icing (page 160) – chocolate
Chocolate-dipped pretzel sticks
3 x chocolate-covered wafer rolls
1 x small Chomp™ chocolate
Large gold balls
White chocolate discs
Round milk chocolates
Chocolate bullets
Rolo® chocolates
Polyester fibre filling

1. Bake the cakes according to the recipe and leave to cool completely.
2. Cut each cake in half across the width so that you have four 150 x 240 mm slabs.
3. Sandwich the four layers together with icing, then coat the entire cake with icing.
4. Cut 11 chocolate-dipped pretzel sticks into 70-mm lengths and place in position at the bottom centre of the cake to make the door. Surround with chocolate-covered wafer rolls to make the doorframe and place a Chomp™ in front of the door for a step.
5. Attach two gold balls for door handles.
6. Arrange the white chocolate discs on the front of the cake as illustrated, cutting in half with a sharp knife where necessary.
7. Refer to the picture to provide two spaces for windows. Cut chocolate-dipped pretzel sticks into five 25-mm lengths for each window and place in position, adding a gold ball for a handle.
8. Place the round milk chocolates in the spaces between the white discs, again cutting to fit as required.
9. Place the chocolate bullets on the front of the roof as illustrated, pressing into the icing to secure. Enhance with gold balls.
10. Decorate the rest of the roof in the same manner as the front of the cake.
11. Use Rolo® chocolates for the chimney stacks, fixing each with a dab of icing. Use three columns of five, four and three, or as preferred. Attach a small puff of polyester filling to the top of each stack for the smoke. (Take care if lighting candles and remove the stacks or the 'smoke' as a precautionary measure.)
12. Decorate the sides of the cake with chocolate discs or leave plain if preferred.

Mesmerizing

SETTING THE SCENE

The enchantment of life beneath the waves, coupled with the fantasy of the mermaids, will ensure that this party will make memories that will last forever. This theme is easily adapted to incorporate a swimming party if the birthday falls during the summer.

* Tie a bunch of turquoise, lilac and silver balloons together with curling ribbon and attach to the front gate to greet the guests.
* Lay a trail of sea sand and seashells from the gate to the front door.
* As guests arrive, present each with a bottle of bubbles so that they may create a sea of bubbles while they wait for the rest of the children to arrive.
* Hang a turquoise organza curtain in the doorway for the children to pass through as they enter the 'Mermaids' Pool'.
* Cover the floor with plenty of turquoise, lilac and silver balloons so that the guests may wade through the sea. Line the windows with turquoise cellophane and hang vertical strips of turquoise and lilac crepe paper, interspersed with ropes of silver tinsel, against the walls.
* Attach cardboard cutouts of fish, mermaids, starfish, sea horses and other sea creatures to the walls.
* Create an ocean canopy above the party table by draping turquoise and lilac streamers from the centre of the ceiling to the outer edges.
* Attach fishing line to plastic spheres, preferably of varying sizes, and suspend these from the ceiling so that they hang over the table at different heights and look like bubbles.
* Create colourful cardboard cutouts of mermaids and suspend these above the table using fishing line.
* Cover the party table with a turquoise cloth or turquoise crepe paper and use a square of silver organza as an overlay. Scatter ocean confetti on the tablecloth and place a few shells and plastic starfish on the table to complete the scene.

Recommended age group: 6–10

Mermaids

INVITATIONS

YOU WILL NEED:

Lilac notepaper

Pen

Lilac, turquoise and silver curling ribbon

Silver plastic oyster shells

Sea sand

Ocean confetti

Small rectangle of lilac board paper for the nametag

Paper punch

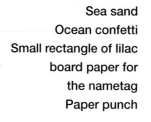

1. Write the invitation details (see Suggested Wording) on the notepaper. Fold up into a small square, tie with ribbon, and place inside the oyster.
2. Add a few grains of clean sea sand and a pinch of confetti to the oyster.
3. Write the guest's name on the nametag, punch a hole in one corner and attach to the ribbon.
4. Pass the ribbon through the back of the oyster so that the card protrudes when the oyster is closed.

SUGGESTED WORDING

Frolic with the mermaids at (child's name)'s party.

Catch the wave on: (date) at (address)

Descend to the floor of the ocean at: (time party starts)

Return to shore: (time party ends)

RSVP: King Neptune's helper at (phone number) before (date)

TREAT BAGS

YOU WILL NEED (PER BAG):

1 x empty 2-litre clear plastic soft drink container

Scissors or craft knife

Paper punch

1 x 300-mm long silver pipe cleaner

Sequins – silver, turquoise and lilac

Craft glue

Silver, lilac and turquoise curling ribbon – each cut into 50–60 mm lengths

Small rectangle of lilac board paper for the nametag

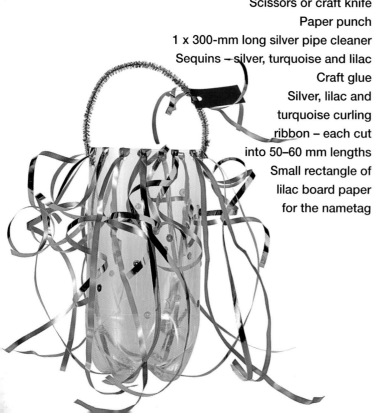

1. Carefully cut the upper section from the container and discard.
2. Mark points around the rim of the container, about 20 mm apart and 5 mm from the rim.
3. Using the points as a guide, carefully punch holes through each marked point.
4. Insert the ends of the pipe cleaner through two opposite holes and twist the ends upwards towards the rim of the container so that the pipe cleaner forms a handle.
5. Use craft glue to randomly attach sequins all over the container.
6. Fold each length of ribbon in half, insert the loop through the hole and make a knot by feeding the tail ends of ribbon through the loop and pulling to secure.
7. Write the guest's name on the nametag and attach to the handle using curling ribbon.

GAMES AND ACTIVITIES

Mermaid Tails

This game is easily adapted for play in a swimming pool.

YOU WILL NEED (PER GUEST):
Length of material or any other binding that is long
 enough to go around the child's knees

Divide the children into two teams and have them stand in a line one behind the other. Bind each child's knees together with the tie.

On starter's orders, the first child in each team must race to a predetermined spot and back to the rest of the team. She must tap the next child in line on the hand and then take up position at the end of the line.

The game continues in this manner until all the children have had a turn and there is a winning team. The winners receive a small prize, the rest receive a token.

Pearl Race

YOU WILL NEED (PER TEAM):
1 x large spoon
2 x bowls or buckets
Small polystyrene balls the size of a golf ball,
 one per child

Divide the children into two or more teams and have each team stand in line one behind the other.

Place an empty bowl/bucket in front of each team. Put the polystyrene balls (the pearls) in the second bowl/bucket and place it a predetermined distance away from each team. Give the first child in each team a spoon.

On starter's orders, the first child in each team runs to the bowl containing the 'pearls', scoops one up and races back to place it in the empty bucket. (This is not an easy task as the balls are light!) If they drop a pearl they must scoop it up again before continuing.

The spoon is then handed to the next child and the game continues until there is a winning team. The winners receive a prize, the rest receive a token.

Find the Pearl

This game may be adapted for the swimming pool: the children must dive to locate the gems in the water. One child per team dives at a time and once they locate a pearl they leave the pool and the next child takes a turn.

YOU WILL NEED (PER TEAM):
1 x tub or similar container large enough for
 children to sit around
Clean sea sand
1 x spoon per child
Fake pearls and other jewels/gems

Fill the container with the sea sand and bury the pearls and gems in the sand.

Divide the children into two or more teams and allow them to search for the pearls in a predetermined time limit. The team that finds the most pearls and jewels is the winner. Winners receive a prize, the rest receive a token, and everyone keeps the gems that they found.

Hungry Octopus

Create a pre-determined safe area (cordon off the area with a length of rope laid along the ground) and appoint one player as the octopus.

The octopus must stand with her back to the children, who must approach her stealthily, all the time asking 'Octopus, octopus, what's the time?'

Without turning around, the octopus must call out any time that she wishes, but when she answers 'Dinnertime!' the octopus must spin around and try to catch someone while the children run to the safe area.

When the octopus catches a child, she remains captive. The octopus and her captive join hands to simulate a tentacle and together they try to nab the next child. (Only the octopus answers to the question though!)

Should the octopus fail to nab a child, then the last one to enter the safe area becomes a captive.

The game continues in the same manner with the tentacle becoming longer and longer until there is only one child left, who is the winner. The winner receives a prize, the rest receive tokens.

PARTY FOOD

Creepy Crab Biscuits

Wafer ice-cream cones
Marie biscuits or Rich Tea™ biscuits
Icing (page 160) – turquoise
Silver balls
Small sweets of choice
Orange apricot sweets, halved
Small orange banana-shaped sweets
Hundreds and thousands

1. Cut about 50 mm from the tip of the cone, slicing at a slight angle. Discard the tip.
2. Coat a Marie biscuit with turquoise icing, and attach the upended cone, pressing gently to secure.
3. Pipe turquoise stars around the base of the cone and enhance with silver balls.
4. Add a few sweets to the inside of the cone.
5. Coat a second biscuit with turquoise icing and attach it to the tip of the cone, using a blob of icing on the underside of the biscuit to secure.
6. Place the apricot sweet, flat side down, in the centre of the biscuit. Attach the banana-shaped sweets and the silver balls as illustrated.
7. Sprinkle lightly with hundreds and thousands.

Awesome Oysters

Meringues (page 161) – yields about 28 oysters
Icing (page 160) – turquoise
Edible turquoise glitter
Large silver balls

1. Prepare the meringue mixture according to the recipe, then use a wide star-shaped nozzle to pipe oval rosettes (about 50–60 mm in length) onto a baking tray lined with greaseproof paper.
2. Bake as directed.
3. Coat the flat side of a meringue with icing and sprinkle with edible glitter. Attach a second meringue, flat side down, leaving the front side open to expose the 'pearl', which is positioned as shown.

Sea Anemone Cupcakes

Ensure that the children remove the balls (anemones) before eating!

Party Cupcakes (page 161)
Silver foil cookie cups (baking cases)
Icing (page 160) – turquoise
Tiny toy balls or large gumballs
Silver edible glitter
Star-shaped sweets

1. Bake the cupcakes in silver foil cookie cups according to the recipe and leave to cool completely before coating with the icing.
2. Place a ball on the top of each cupcake and sprinkle edible glitter over the icing. If using gumballs, attach icing spikes by using the pull-out motion with the writing nozzle. Decorate with star sweets.

Mermaid Princess Biscuits

Easy Biscuits (page 161)
Mermaid template (page 165)
Icing (page 160) – flesh-coloured, turquoise, yellow, red
Turquoise edible glitter
Turquoise balls
Small turquoise star-shaped sweets

1. Prepare the biscuit dough as per the recipe.
2. Trace the template onto stiff cardboard, cut it out and use to cut out the biscuits. Bake as directed and leave to cool completely.
3. Coat the upper half of the biscuit with flesh-coloured icing and define the arms and the chin, using a toothpick to make the lines.
4. Use the star nozzle to pipe the mermaid tail in turquoise, finishing the fin section with a pull-out motion. Sprinkle the tail with glitter glue.
5. Pipe two stars for the bikini top. Ice the hair as illustrated and enhance with a star-shaped sweet.
6. Place the turquoise balls in position for the eyes and pipe a mouth with red icing.

MERMAID CASTLE CAKE

3 x Basic Cake (page 160) – two x 280 mm round cakes, and the third mixture divided and baked in three greased and lined, large-sized food cans (±750 g size), to create three tube cakes for the turrets
±400 g white baking chocolate
Turquoise powdered food colouring
±500 g unsalted peanuts
Icing (page 160) – turquoise
Wooden skewers
Sugar paste
Lilac powdered food colouring, for doors, windows and stars

Large silver balls
3 x wafer ice-cream cones
Hundreds and thousands
Small silver balls
Turquoise edible glitter
Small silver bell
Prestik® or Blu-tac™
Silver cord or small chain, about 50 mm long
Toothpick covered with foil
Lilac lollipops
Mermaids, ocean scene toys and star-shaped sweets
Florist's wire

1. Bake the cakes as directed and leave to cool completely.
2. Melt the chocolate according to the manufacturer's directions and mix in the turquoise colouring before adding the peanuts, stirring well to coat. Drop clusters onto a baking sheet lined with greaseproof paper and leave to set in the fridge. (You can make these a few days in advance to save time.)
3. Sandwich the large rounds cakes on top of each other with icing and coat the top and the sides as well. Swirl the icing on the top of the cake to create a wavy appearance. Position the peanut clusters around the sides of the cake. (You may wish to add them to the top of the cake as well for a rocky appearance, but only do this once you have placed the towers in position.)
4. Level the tops of the tube cakes by cutting with a serrated knife. Cut about 30 mm from the top of one of the tube cakes and attach to another with a layer of icing. You should now have three turrets measuring about 130 mm, 100 mm and 70 mm in height. Place the tallest turret in position in the centre back section of the cake, inserting one or two wooden skewers to secure. Coat with icing, again swirling the surface to create a wavy appearance. Place the shorter turrets on either side, slightly forward, once more securing with skewers. Coat with icing using the same technique as for the larger roll.
5. Colour the sugar paste with the lilac colouring. Roll out the sugar paste to 2–4 mm thick on a surface dusted with icing sugar and cut out the door and windows. The door measures 70 x 40 mm, the three parallel windows are 40 x 20 mm and the side tower windows are 30 x 40 mm. Use a small icing nozzle or star-shaped cutter to make the holes for the windowpanes. Position as illustrated.
6. Coat the ice-cream cones with icing and cover with hundreds and thousands. Place one on top of each tower. Use the star nozzle to pipe a row of stars around the base of each cone. Decorate the stars with small silver balls. Pipe a star on the tip of each cone and add a large silver ball.
7. Brush the entire cake with edible glitter
8. Attach a small piece of Prestik® to the inside of the bell and secure the chain or cord. Place the bell on one end of the toothpick and insert the free end into the cake, next to the door of the main tower.
9. Press out star shapes from the sugar paste with a small star cutter and lay a starry path to the front door. Attach extra stars to the tower walls.
10. Place the lollipops in front of the castle.
11. Decorate the rest of the cake using mermaids and toys as preferred. Attach fish, turtles, and so on to florist's wire with Prestik® and insert into the cake so that they may swim around this delightful underwater scene.

SETTING THE SCENE

This theme is fabulous if the birthday falls around the start of the birthday child's first school year. It also works well at the end of a long school holiday, as this is an ideal way to reconnect with schoolmates! Adapt the ideas and use without the birthday component for a fun get-together for the class.

* Attach red and yellow balloons, tied together with red and yellow curling ribbon, to the front gate.
* Make a cardboard sign that reads (child's surname)'s School and decorate it with glitter glue, red and yellow balloons and ribbons. Attach the sign to the front entrance.
* Place a table in the entrance with a sign saying 'Teacher'. Place an apple and a pile of books on the table together with a ruler and other items of stationery. Include a globe of the world if you have one. Have the guests place their gifts here as they arrive.
* Cover the party table with red crepe paper. Make yellow cardboard numbers, decorate with glitter glue and place on the table. Sprinkle yellow confetti over the paper.
* Make black cardboard posters and use white craft paint to decorate some with stick figure drawings and others with sums. Attach the posters to the walls in the party area.
* School blazers, ties, caps, sports' clothes, and so on may be hung against the walls in the party area, as well as throughout the rest of the house. Mount school photographs decorated with curling ribbon and rosettes against the wall.
* Create a canopy above the party table using twisted red and yellow streamers draped from the centre of the ceiling to the outer edges. Attach red and yellow balloons to the corners of the ceiling.
* Make red and yellow cardboard letters of the alphabet, decorate with glitter glue and suspend from the ceiling above the party table with fishing line so that they hang at varying heights.
* Ring a bell at the start and end of various activities throughout the duration of the party.

Recommended age group: 5–8

First day at School

INVITATIONS

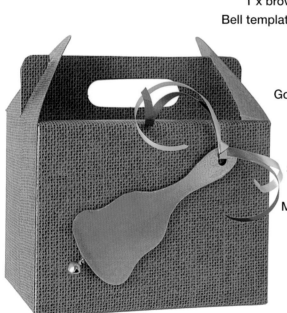

YOU WILL NEED (PER INVITATION):

Bell template (page 165)
Pencil
Stiff cardboard
Scissors
Gold non-toxic craft spray
Yellow notepaper, 100 mm square
Red and yellow curling ribbon
Prestik® or Blu-tac™
Small, round gold bell
Gold cord, 50 mm long
Masking tape
Yellow board paper for
nametag, 60 x 25 mm
Paper punch

1. Enlarge the bell template and trace it onto the cardboard. Cut out. Coat the front of the bell with the gold paint and set aside to dry.
2. Write the invitation details (see Suggested Wording) on the notepaper, roll it up and tie with ribbon. Attach the paper to the back of the bell with Prestik® so that it is not visible from the front.
3. Tie the round bell onto the cord and attach it with masking tape to the back of the cardboard bell, near the lower edge, so that the round bell protrudes.
4. Write the guest's name on the yellow board paper, punch a hole near one corner edge and attach the tag to the neck of the bell with the ribbon.

SUGGESTED WORDING

Heed the bell and come on over to (child's name)'s birthday party!
Catch the school bus on: (date) to (address)
Lessons start: (time party starts)
School ends: (time party ends)
RSVP: The Teacher at (phone number) before (date)
Dress: As for school

TREAT BAGS

YOU WILL NEED (PER BAG):

1 x brown party box
Bell template (page 165)
Pencil
Cardboard
Scissors
Gold non-toxic
craft spray
Gold cord,
50 mm long
Small, round
gold bell
Masking tape

Paper punch
Red and yellow curling ribbon
Craft glue
Felt-tip marker

1. Adjust the template so that the bell measures about 100 mm in length. Trace it onto the cardboard, cut out and coat with the gold paint. Set aside to dry.
2. Attach the gold cord to the bell and fix to the back of the cardboard bell with masking tape.
3. Punch a hole near the end of the handle of the bell, attach the curling ribbon, and glue to the front of the party box.
4. Write the guest's name on the back or on top of the box.

GAMES AND ACTIVITIES

Teacher, Teacher!

A child is chosen to be the teacher. On starter's orders, the teacher leads the group, who must walk behind and in unison ask: 'Teacher, teacher, what's the time?' The teacher, without turning around, answers 'One o'clock', or any randomly selected time. The game continues in this manner with the children traipsing behind the teacher.

When the teacher replies 'Homework time!', he or she spins around to face the children, who must fall to the ground and remain sitting motionless. The last child to sit down is eliminated.

The game continues until there is a winner, who receives a prize. The rest receive tokens.

Teacher's Test

YOU WILL NEED:
Large tea tray
School stationery items such as a sharpener,
    eraser, ruler, mini notebook, crayon, sticker,
    pencil, and so on*

Display the items on the tray and instruct the children to study them for 1 minute. The children must then close their eyes while you remove one item from the tray. The children must identify the item that has been removed. The first child who offers the correct answer receives that particular item and then leaves the game. Reduce the observation period by a few seconds with each round. At the end of the game each child should have received a small prize.

* Ensure that there are sufficient items for the number of guests. If you have to duplicate the items, they should be of varying colours and/or shapes.

Detention Tag

YOU WILL NEED:
Playing area with pre-determined boundaries.

One child is the teacher. The rest of the children move about in the playing area while the teacher attempts to tag them. As a child is tagged they have to remain frozen in place with their legs astride. Children may be released from detention if one of their untagged mates crawls through their legs. If the child who is attempting this is tagged, he or she must remain frozen in place as well. Children who step out of the playing area are also frozen in detention. The game continues until there is one untagged child remaining. The winner and teacher each receive a prize, and the rest receive tokens.

Report Card Blues

YOU WILL NEED:
1 x container holding cards detailing forfeits or prizes
1 x container holding small prizes

Have the children sit in a circle and call out their names in alphabetical order. As each child is called, they must select a note from the container and follow the instructions written on it.

Examples may be: 'Forgot to do homework – hop around the outer circle on one leg'; 'Chattered during lessons – bark like a dog'; 'Top of the class – choose a prize'; 'Failed history test – sing a song'; 'Brought teacher an apple – choose a prize'.

When each child has had a turn, allow those who had to act out forfeits to choose a small token.

PARTY FOOD

Party Pencils

Wafer biscuits
Icing (page 160) – yellow
Fruit-flavoured jelly twists – 3 x 70 mm
    different-coloured lengths per treat
Gold balls

1. Coat the biscuits with yellow icing.
2. Trim one end of each twist to 'sharpen the pencil' and arrange side by side on the wafer biscuit.
3. Place a gold ball in the icing in front of each point.

Alphabet Cones

Use letters that represent the guests' initials or to spell out the name of the birthday child.

Flat-bottomed wafer ice-cream cones
Small sweets of choice
Marie biscuits or Rich Tea™ biscuits
Icing (page 160) – red
Plastic alphabet letters
Gold balls

1. Fill the wafer cone with sweets.
2. Coat the Marie or tea biscuit with icing and place over the open end of the cone. Upend so that the biscuit forms the base.
3. Use the star nozzle to cover the flat top of the upended cone with iced stars and place a letter on top.
4. Pipe a spiral of stars around the cone, finishing with a row around the base of the cone. Decorate with gold balls.

Tasty Rides

Easy Biscuits (page 161)
Bus cookie cutter or template (page 165)
Icing (page 160) – red
Liquorice Allsorts Mini™ squares
Small silver balls
Yellow Smarties®
Red edible glitter

1. Prepare the biscuit dough as per the recipe.
2. Use the cookie cutter or template to cut out the biscuits and bake as directed.
3. Leave biscuits to cool completely before covering with icing.
4. Place the liquorice squares in position for the windows, shaping the front one slightly to follow the contour of the bus.
5. Decorate with silver balls for a headlamp and the doors and position the Smarties® for the wheels. Sprinkle with edible glitter.

School Bells

Marie biscuits or Rich Tea™ biscuits
Icing (page 160) – yellow
Sweetie Pies® or Tunnock's Tea Cakes™
Chocolate-covered wafer rolls
Gold balls

1. Cover the top of the Marie biscuit with icing and position the Sweetie Pie® in the centre.
2. Use a sharp knife to cut a hole in the top of the Sweetie Pie® and insert the chocolate roll into the hole.
3. Use the star nozzle to pipe a row of stars to neaten the hole and conceal any cracks in the chocolate. Decorate with gold balls.
4. Pipe a row of stars around the base of the bell.

LITTLE RED SCHOOL BUS CAKE

1 x Basic Cake (page 160) – 300 x 240 mm

Icing (page 160) – red

5 x small dolls

3 x wafer biscuits

1 x round ring sweet

1 x clear disposable plastic container, measuring ± 220 x 140 mm

4 x small yellow sweets

Small silver balls

4 x flat round sweets

6 x small round sweets

1 x liquorice cable

2 x star-shaped sweets

2 x 150 mm lengths of liquorice straps

4 x round chocolate-coated biscuits

4 x large silver balls

1. Bake the cake according to the recipe and leave to cool completely.
2. Cut the cake in half across the width and sandwich the two halves one on top of the other with a layer of icing.
3. Coat the entire cake with red icing.
4. Cover the lower half of the dolls' bodies with foil and insert into the top of the cake so that there is a driver and four passengers.
5. Cut the wafer biscuits into 25 mm widths and insert one piece behind each doll for a back rest.
6. Place the round ring sweet in front of the driver for the steering wheel.
7. Place the plastic container upside down over the dolls to create the top of the bus.
8. Coat the 'roof' with a light layer of icing and edge with a row of piped stars to neaten.
9. Pipe stars around the base of the plastic container to neaten.
10. Use the star nozzle to pipe window borders and two doors on either side of the bus, as illustrated. Add the small yellow sweets to make door handles.
11. Mark the outline of the front grille with a toothpick and place the small silver balls in position using a small pair of tweezers.
12. For the lights, attach the flat round sweets to the front and back of the bus. Add the small round sweets as indicators. Attach the liquorice cable for the exhaust.
13. Position the star-shaped sweet emblems at the front and back of the bus.
14. Use the liquorice straps to create the front and rear bumpers.
15. Attach the biscuits for the wheels. Use a dab of icing to attach a large silver ball to the centre of each biscuit. Use the star nozzle to pipe mudguards around each wheel as illustrated.

UPSIDE DOWN

SETTING THE SCENE

From FINISH to START the children will have so much fun at this party!
The possibilities are endless and may be incorporated into any of the other themes.

* Attach a sign to the gate saying 'EYBDOOG'. Decorate with lime green and orange ribbons, balloons and glitter glue and hang it upside down. Greet guests at the gate and hand out lime green and orange stickers with their names written on back to front. They must use these names for the entire party and must walk backwards into the party area. Mark the front door with an upside down 'TIXE' sign.

* Throughout the house have objects in an upside down or back to front position, for example chairs may be placed facing away from the tables. Pictures and photographs may be turned back to front. Place flowers in see through vases with the blossoms in the water and the stems protruding.

* Cover the floor with lime and orange twisted streamers arranged from the centre to the edges. Place a lime tablecloth in the centre of the room, so that the streamers protrude from under the cloth. Place the table over the cloth and decorate the legs with lime and orange curling ribbon. Sprinkle orange confetti over the cloth. Set out the food beneath the table so that the children will have to crawl to reach the snacks. Serve sweets and chips on small platters covered with upended bowls.

* Tie bunches of lime green and orange balloons together with curling ribbon. Place bundles on the floor in each corner of the room. Suspend plastic or cardboard animals and snakes from the ceiling with fishing line so that they 'fly'. Plastic or cardboard birds, bats, and so on should be placed on the floor.

* Write the words of the 'Happy Birthday' song back to front on a poster and mount in the party area so that the guests may sing this version to the birthday child.

Recommended age group: 7-12

INVITATIONS

YOU WILL NEED (PER INVITATION):
Lime green board paper – 100 mm square
Glitter pen
1 x small mirror (necessary to read
the invitation details!)
Prestik® or Blu-tac™
Lime green board paper
for nametag – 60 x 25 mm
Paper punch
Orange and lime green
curling ribbon

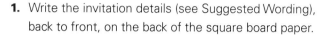

1. Write the invitation details (see Suggested Wording), back to front, on the back of the square board paper.
2. Attach the mirror to the centre front of the board paper using a small blob of Prestik®.
3. Write the guest's name backwards on the nametag.
4. Punch a hole in one corner of the invitation and another near a side edge of the nametag.
5. Thread the ribbon through the holes to attach the nametag to the invitation.

SUGGESTED WORDING

Turn the world upside down on (date)
Walk back to front to: (child's name)'s party
Upside down house: (address)
Be topsy-turvy from: (time party starts) to
(time party ends)
RSVP: The upside-down lady at (phone number)
before (date)
Dress: Back to front and upside down!

TREAT BAGS

The treats should be attached to the OUTSIDE of this upside-down treat container!

YOU WILL NEED:
Small white plastic buckets
Felt-tip marker
Twirling windmill toys (remove the plastic handle
to attach and distribute at the end of the party)
Prestik® or Blu-tac™
Sweets and party favours of choice
Lime green and orange curling ribbon

1. Write the guest's name on the lid of the bucket and turn the bucket upside down.
2. Attach the twirling windmill toy to the 'top' of the bucket with Prestik® and surround with sweets and favours of choice.
3. Tie curling ribbon around the base of the windmill to enhance.

GAMES AND ACTIVITIES

BACK-TO-FRONT MUSICAL FREEZE

YOU WILL NEED:
Music

Have the children dance about. When the music STARTS they must freeze on the spot. The last child to stop moving is eliminated. When the music STOPS they must dance about once more. The game continues in this manner, with one child being eliminated in each round, until only one child remains. The first child to have been eliminated wins the prize (don't divulge this information until the end of the game!) while the actual winner (the last child) gets second prize. The rest receive tokens.

TREASURE HIDE

YOU WILL NEED (PER TEAM):
1 x bag containing an equal number of
   colour-coded stones
1 x list of clues pin-pointing the various
   hiding places

Divide the children into two or more teams. Present each team with their bag of colour-coded stones and instruct them to follow the clues to the various hiding places for each of the stones. On starter's orders, the teams must set out to hide their stones. The first team to return to the starting point after successfully hiding their stones in the relevant spots is the winner, but the LAST team in wins the prize! The rest of the children receive tokens.

WRAP THE PARCEL

YOU WILL NEED:
1 x prize
Several (amount as preferred) sheets of wrapping
   paper large enough to cover the parcel
1 x reel of adhesive tape
Music

Have the children sit in a circle, with the paper and adhesive tape in the centre, and pass the prize from one to the other until the music starts. The child who is holding the present on the first beat of the music must wrap the present in a layer of paper. Once he has finished, the music stops and the present is passed around again until the music starts once more.

The game continues in this manner with the present being wrapped in all the layers of paper. The child who wraps the last layer is the winner and gets to keep the prize, the rest receive tokens.

BALLOON SQUEEZE

YOU WILL NEED:
Inflated balloons, each team starts with one
   but extras should be provided

Divide the children into two or more teams and have them line up one behind the other. On starter's orders, the first child in each team places a balloon between his knees and runs backwards to a predetermined point and then returns to the starting point. The balloon is handed to the next child in line, who repeats the procedure. The game continues until all have had a turn. The winning team is the one that finishes first, having used the least amount of balloons, but of course the last team in will win the prize! The rest receive tokens.

PARTY FOOD

PERFECT HANDSTANDS

Wafer biscuits
Handstand template (page 165)
Icing (page 160) – orange, white, lime green
Sour hand- and feet-shaped sweets
White chocolate discs
Chocolate chips
Non-toxic red food colouring pen
Silver balls

1. Use a serrated knife and the template to shape the wafer biscuit.
2. Coat with orange icing and attach the hands and feet as shown.
3. Place the chocolate disc in position for the head.
4. Attach two chocolate chips for the eyes. Use the writing nozzle and white icing to make the pupils. Draw the mouth with the pen (or use red food colouring diluted in a drop of water or white alcohol).
5. Use the writing nozzle and green icing to pull out strands of hair. Decorate the body with silver balls.

OUTSIDE-IN ICE CREAM

Prepare these well in advance and serve with plenty of serviettes!

Marie biscuits or Rich Tea™ biscuits
Icing (page 160) – colour to match ice cream
Flake®
Wafer ice-cream cones
Ice cream – white, or coloured with powdered food colouring
Astros™ or Skittles™
Serviettes

1. Lightly coat the top of a Marie biscuit with icing.
2. Place a Flake® inside an ice cream cone and upend onto the biscuit. Press gently to secure.
3. Coat the outside of the cone with ice cream, covering the entire surface with a generous layer. Place in the freezer until required. Dot with Astros™ and distribute to guests along with a few serviettes.

DOG HOTS!

Hot dog rolls
Butter or margarine
Hot dog sausages
Clear plastic cocktail sticks
Tomato sauce in a squeeze bottle
Mustard in a squeeze bottle
Styrofoam® hot dog food trays
Serviettes

1. Cut the hot dog rolls down their length, taking care not to cut right through. Butter as preferred and then close again by pressing the two halves together.
2. Cut the sausages in half down their length and attach one half to each of the sides of the roll, securing them with cocktail sticks.
3. Create squiggles of tomato sauce and mustard along the length of the roll.
4. Serve on top of a foam hot dog food tray with a serviette.

TOPSY-TURVY CUPCAKES

Party Cupcakes (page 161)
Silver foil cookie cups (baking cases)
Icing (page 160) – orange
Marie biscuits or Rich Tea™ biscuits
Silver balls
Small plastic candleholders
Birthday candles

1. Bake the cupcakes in the foil cookie cups according to the recipe and leave to cool completely.
2. Use a serrated knife to trim the cupcake if necessary so that the top is level. Cover with icing.
3. Coat the top of a Marie biscuit with icing, then place the cupcake upside down on top of the biscuit, pressing down to secure.
4. Use the star nozzle to pipe a row of stars on the edge of the Marie biscuit to neaten.
5. Decorate with silver balls.
6. Push the candleholder into the centre of the upturned cupcake and place the candle in position.

SPOT THE MISTAKE CAKE

I have illustrated a few examples of toys that may be used for this 'spot the mistake' cake,
but make it as busy as you can while your imagination goes upside down!

2 x Basic Cake (page 160) – two 300 x 240 mm cakes
Icing (page 160) – blue, green
Various toys, as preferred

1. Bake the cakes as per the recipe and leave to cool completely.
2. Place the cakes alongside each other with the longer sides joined together. Secure the join with a layer of icing.
3. Use a toothpick to mark a boundary diagonally across the cake to separate the sea from the land.
4. Cover the sea with blue icing and roughen up the surface with the point of the knife.
5. Coat the land with a thin layer of green icing and then use the star nozzle to cover completely.
6. Allow the birthday child to help with the arrangement of the toys as you place all sea creatures and water activities on the land and vice versa. If preferred, you may also place some of the articles upside down.

WRESTLING

SETTING THE SCENE

All little champs will love the opportunity to emulate their heroes!

* Enlarge the template of the title belt (page 163) and trace it onto stiff cardboard. Use black and gold non-toxic craft spray to decorate and attach the belt to the front gate to easily identify the party venue. Include a bunch of black, red and white balloons if preferred.

* Make sports pennants from felt fabric and attach them to thin dowel sticks with craft glue. Insert the pennants in plant pots and other garden containers. If you wish, make one for each guest, which they may take home at the end of the party. Use a felt-tip marker to write their names on the front of the pennant and decorate as preferred.

* Set up a ticket booth at the party entrance where guests should redeem their 'tickets' (the invitations) for a tattoo stamp that permits entry to the party area. Enlist the help of a friend to man this booth and don't fret if a queue builds up, after all that's usual for a wrestling event!

* Cover the table with black, red and white crepe paper strips and top with wrestling figurines. Create a canopy by draping twisted black, red and white streamers from the centre of the ceiling to the edges.

* Place posters of wrestling heroes on the walls. Cut store-bought cone-shaped party hats in half along their length and attach to the posters to allow the wrestling idols to join in the spirit of the party!

* Suspend gold cardboard medals from the ceiling with fishing line and hang at varying heights above the table. Guests may take one home at the end of the party.

* Tie bundles of black, red and white balloons in strategic positions all about the party area.

* Cordon off the play area using four corner posts to create a square. Tie three 'ropes' around the posts using construction tape or crepe paper streamers. Arrange seating around the ring.

* Enlarge a picture of a wrestling star to a size that would be appropriate for the children. Attach to a sturdy piece of cardboard and remove the face area using a craft knife. Have the children stand behind this with their faces in the hole and take photographs. Ask a helper to process the photos on a home computer or deliver to a one-hour photo lab so that they are ready for the children to take home.

Recommended age group: 6-10

FEVER!

INVITATIONS

YOU WILL NEED (PER INVITATION):
White board paper – 150 x 80 mm
Glitter pen
Red board paper (for the folder) – 180 x 180 mm
Craft glue
Black gift ribbon – 180 mm long
Paper punch
Red board paper (for the nametag) –
60 mm x 25 mm
Large gold confetti circle
Thin gold cord – 120 mm long
Prestik® or Blu-tac™

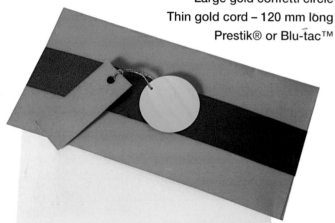

1. Write the party details (see Suggested Wording) on the white board paper.
2. To make the folder, fold the red board paper in half and glue the sides only. Leave the top open, thus creating a neat folder for the ticket.
3. Slide the party details into the folder.
4. Paste the ribbon on to the front of the folder using craft glue.
5. Write the guest's name on the nametag, punch a hole near a side edge and attach it to the gold circle with the cord.
6. Attach the gold circle to the centre of the ribbon with a blob of Prestik®.

SUGGESTED WORDING

(Child's name) Birthday Championship Title Bout!
Admit One to the Main Arena on: (date)
Stadium: (address)
Ticket Office Opens: (time party starts)
Ticket Office Closes: (time party ends)
RSVP: The referee at (phone number) before (date)
Dress: As your favourite wrestler!

TREAT BAGS

YOU WILL NEED (PER BAG):
1 x brown paper packet
Black gift ribbon – about 600 mm, depending on the size of the bag used
Stapler
Paper punch
Red board paper – 60 mm x 25 mm
Glitter pen
Large gold confetti circle
Thin gold cord – 120 mm long
Prestik® or Blu-tac™

1. Fold the top of the paper bag over twice to close.
2. Wrap the ribbon around the bag and staple the ends together at the back.
3. Punch a hole in the centre of one side edge of the nametag and write the guest's name with the glitter pen. Punch a hole in the gold circle and attach the nametag with the cord.
4. Attach the gold circle to the centre of the ribbon with a blob of Prestik®.

GAMES AND ACTIVITIES

WRESTLE OF STRENGTH

YOU WILL NEED:

1 x length of rope*, tied with a knot in the middle or
   marked with ribbon

Chalk or tape to make a centre mark in the play area,
   as well as two lines, equidistant from this on either
   side, as the starting line for each team

Divide the children into two teams, ensuring that their
weights are evenly distributed. Have them stand one
behind the other, with the team leader behind the
team's starting mark. The children must grasp the rope
firmly, then, on starter's orders, they must try to pull
the opposing team over the centre mark. The winning
team receives a prize, the rest receive tokens.

* The length will be determined by the number of
guests, but the rope should be long enough to allow
1 metre of free space on either side of the centre
point, with an additional 500 mm of rope per child.

SILENTLY NIMBLE

YOU WILL NEED:

1 x duvet or similar
4–5 small squeaky rubber toys
2 x blindfolds
Music

Spread the duvet on the ground of the playing area
and randomly hide the squeaky toys beneath it.
Divide the children into two teams and blindfold the
first child in line of each team. On starter's orders,
both blindfolded children must step onto the duvet
and move about in time to the music. The first child to
step on a squeaker is eliminated. The music stops
while he leaves the play area, removes his blindfold
and tags the next child, who then dons the blindfold
and repeats the procedure when the music starts. The
winning side is the one with the most 'untagged'
children. (You may need to reposition the squeakers if
the children become familiar with their whereabouts.)
The winners earn a prize, the rest receive tokens.

RUMBLING ROYAL RUMPUS

YOU WILL NEED:

Balloons (a different colour for each team
   and sufficient for each child on the team,
   plus a few extra)

String for the balloons – 80–100 cm per balloon

String, tape or chalk to demarcate a playing area

Music

Inflate the balloons and tie with string. Divide the
children into two teams, and give each a balloon in
their team's colour, which they must tie to their left
ankles. Have three children from each team enter the
playing area. When the music starts, the children
must jump about and attempt to pop the balloon tied
to an opposing team member's ankle. As soon as a
balloon is popped, that child must quickly leave the
playing area and tag the next team member, who
must enter the 'ring' and continue the quest to
eliminate the rivals.

   Play continues until the children that are left in the
ring are all from the same team. The winning team
receives a prize, the rest receive tokens. The child
who has been in the ring the longest may receive an
additional prize!

THE WINNER'S PURSE

YOU WILL NEED:

Music

1 x small bag containing coins (amount optional)

Have the children stand in a circle. When the music
starts, the bag must be passed from one wrestler to
another. The wrestler must take the bag in his left
hand, put his left arm behind his back, and then lift
his right arm over his right shoulder to retrieve the
bag from behind his back. The bag must then be
passed to the next wrestler. The bag is passed in this
wriggling fashion until the music stops. The wrestler
who is holding the bag is eliminated. Play continues
in this manner until one child is left. The winner
receives the bag of coins, the rest receive tokens.

PARTY FOOD

Apart from the food ideas mentioned below and in keeping with the atmosphere of a wrestling arena, you may consider providing hot dogs with sauces, served from a food kiosk in foam hot dog containers with lids.

WAVING HANDS

Cardboard inner tubes from kitchen paper towels
Red non-toxic craft spray
Popcorn (½ cup unpopped corn will make enough
  to fill about 3 gloves)
Disposable clear plastic food gloves
Broad adhesive packaging tape
Elastic bands
Red and white curling ribbon

1. Paint the cardboard tubes red and set aside to dry.
2. Make the popcorn as per the packet instructions and leave to cool before filling the gloves. You may wish to vary the finger positions – push the unfilled fingers to the inside of the glove, knot them together to keep them in place, and fill the rest of the glove with the popcorn.
3. Seal one end of the cardboard tube with the adhesive tape (to prevent the popcorn falling through) and insert the sealed end into the hand. Cuff the glove around the tube and tie tightly with the elastic band so that the hand is supported securely.
4. Tie ribbon around the 'wrist' to cover the elastic.

MIGHTY MEAN MASKS

Party Cupcakes (page 161)
Silver foil cookie cups (baking cases)
Icing (page 160) – black
Red Mini Astros™ sweets
Liquorice Allsorts Mini™ sweets
Straight white sweets

1. Bake the cupcakes in the cookie cups as per the recipe and leave to cool completely.
2. Ice the top of the cupcake with black icing.
3. Place the Mini Astros™ in position for the eyes. Trim the white layer of the Liquorice Allsorts Mini™ to make the nose and the trimmings of the mask. Use a straight white sweet for the mouth.

THE TITLE BELT

Easy Biscuits (page 161)
Title belt template (page 163)
Icing (page 160) – black
Gold foil-covered chocolate coins
Small gold balls

1. Prepare the biscuit dough as per the recipe.
2. Use the title belt template to cut out the biscuits and bake as directed. Leave to cool completely before covering the entire biscuit with black icing.
3. Place the gold coin in the centre of the biscuit and use the star nozzle to pipe a row of stars around the coin.
4. Decorate the belt with the gold balls as illustrated.

CHAMPION TREATS

Flat-bottomed wafer ice-cream cones
Small sweets of choice
Marie biscuits or Rich Tea™ biscuits
Icing (page 160) – white
Liquorice straps
Gold foil-covered chocolate coins
Small toy wrestlers
Small gold balls

1. Fill the cone with sweets.
2. Coat the top of the Marie biscuit with icing and place over the open end of the cone. Upend so that the biscuit forms the base.
3. Trail a strip of icing from the top of the cone to the base and attach a liquorice strap, trimming to fit. Press gently to secure.
4. Place a dab of icing on the back of the gold coin and attach it to the centre of the strap.
5. Use the star nozzle to pipe a row of stars around the base of the cone and on the top.
6. Place the wrestler on top of the cone and decorate with the gold balls as shown.

CHAMPIONSHIP TOURNAMENT CAKE

2 x Basic Cake (page 160) – 2 x 250 mm square cakes
Icing (page 160) – white, red, black
250 g sugar paste
4 x long, straight, multi-coloured lollipops (approximate length including stick – 200 mm)
Decorative red cord – allow about 3 metres
Prestik® or Blu-tac™
2 x toy wrestlers

1. Bake the cakes as directed and leave to cool completely.
2. Sandwich the two cakes together with a layer of white icing and use a serrated knife to level the top if necessary.
3. Coat the top with a thin layer of smooth icing as a base for the sugar paste. Roll out the sugar paste to 2–4 mm thick on a surface that has been dusted with icing sugar. Carefully place the sugar paste on the cake so that it covers the top.
4. Very gently insert a lollipop into each corner, about 25 mm from the edge, taking care not to crumble the edges of the cake.
5. Attach the cord with a small blob of Prestik® to the back of one of the back lollipops (ensure that it is hidden from the front view) and wind it around the outside of each lollipop to form a barrier. Join the free end to the starting point by wedging it into the blob of Prestik®. Repeat so that you have three barrier ropes.
6. Decorate the sides of the cake with red and black icing as shown – use a ruler to mark guide lines.
7. Place the wrestlers in position on the top of the cake, securing with a dab of icing if necessary.

SETTING THE SCENE

'When I grow up I want to be ...' Give guests the opportunity to live their dreams with this theme that makes fancy dress a piece of cake!

- ❖ Use white board paper, A3 size, and roll up like a diploma. Tie with a bright blue ribbon and attach to the front gate together with a bunch of white and blue balloons that have been tied together with blue trailing ribbons.
- ❖ Use blue stiff cardboard squares to make mortarboards. Make tassels by plaiting strips of crepe paper and secure them to the mortarboards with round paper fasteners. Make these in varying sizes and attach to the walls in the party area.
- ❖ Attach posters depicting various professions to the walls.
- ❖ Cover the party table with a white cloth and make large blue rosettes from crepe paper to attach to the tablecloth. Sprinkle blue confetti on the table and decorate with short curls of blue curling ribbon.
- ❖ Use white and blue twisted streamers to create a canopy effect above the party table by draping the streamers from the centre of the ceiling to the outer edges.
- ❖ Make a special diploma for each guest that they may take home after the party – 'This diploma is awarded to (guest's name) for attending (birthday child's name)'s special day on (date). With special thanks for contributing to the fun.' Place these on the table and throughout the party area.
- ❖ Suspend white and blue balloons in bundles from the corners of the ceiling and in strategic positions throughout the party area.
- ❖ Place any trophies that may be available, or buy toy plastic ones from party supply outlets, on the table. The trophies may be used for serving sweets.

Recommended age group: 5–10

CAREER
CAPERS

INVITATIONS

YOU WILL NEED (PER INVITATION):

1 x page white A4 notepaper
Blue felt-tip marker
Elastic band
1 x 240 mm length of blue ribbon
Craft glue
1 x blue board paper disc, 35 mm in diameter
Blue glitter

1. Write the invitation details (see Suggested Wording) on the notepaper and roll up to resemble a diploma. Use an elastic band to assist with the process – only remove when complete.
2. Cut the ribbon in half, then wind one half around the diploma overlapping the ends slightly. Glue to secure.
3. To make the rosette, cut the remaining ribbon in half again – you should have two 60 mm lengths. Neaten the ends and glue the ribbons to the centre back of the disc so that they extend as illustrated. Coat the front of the paper disc with glue and cover with glitter.
4. Leave to dry before attaching to the diploma, on top of the ribbon, with a dab of glue.
5. Write the guest's name on the back of the diploma with the marker. Remove the elastic band.

SUGGESTED WORDING

Graduate at (child's name)'s birthday party
Receive your degree on: (date)
Campus: (address)
Capping ceremony: (duration of party)
RSVP: The Dean at (phone number) before (date)
Dress: As your chosen career

TREAT BAGS

YOU WILL NEED:

Rosettes, as per the invitation
Craft glue
White party boxes
Blue felt-tip marker

1. Make a rosette as per the invitation instructions and attach to the front side of the party box with craft glue.
2. Write the guest's name on the back of the box.

GAMES AND ACTIVITIES

Games may be adapted according to the professions that you prefer. The winner in each category receives a prize together with a diploma (as per the invitation) for being the top achiever! The following are a few examples.

FIREMAN - DOUSE THE FLAMES!

YOU WILL NEED (PER TEAM):
3 large, sturdy candles
Water pistol
Bucket of water (for refilling water pistols)
Blackboard to record scores

Place the three candles on a table in an area without drafts. Divide the children into two teams and instruct them to stand in line, one behind the other, with the first child standing behind a mark measured a fair distance from the candles (distance depends on age group). The candles are lit and each child has a turn to douse each of the three flames with only one squirt per flame. Water pistols are refilled as necessary.

The points are recorded and the team with the most successful squirts wins a prize plus a diploma, the other team receives tokens.

FASHION DESIGNER - DRESS A MODEL

YOU WILL NEED (PER TEAM):
A black bag containing:
Pieces of fabric (large enough to drape
   around the body)
Safety pins
Shoes, handbags, jewellery, wigs, make up,
   and other accessories of choice
Crepe paper

Divide the children into small groups. Each group is given a bag of supplies and sent off to a room to 'work'. A model is elected by the children to represent each group, and then the children must set to work within a predetermined time frame to adorn their model with the items in their bag. A fashion parade is held and the children choose the winner. The winning group receives a prize as well as a diploma; the remaining children receive tokens.

COMPUTER SPECIALIST - INSTALL THE SYSTEM

This game is played like a beetle drive.

YOU WILL NEED (PER TEAM):
A card for each child
Glue stick
Dice
Small zip lock bag for each child containing
   cutout drawings of:
A computer (CPU) (six)
Monitor (five)
Keyboard (four)
Mouse (three)
Mouse pad (two)
Printer (one)

Divide the children into small groups.

Each number on the dice represents a different part of the system (see above) and each child has to throw a six to start 'installing their system'.

Each child throws the dice in turn and the game continues with the children building onto their system with the appropriate throw of the dice, in descending order, as depicted above.

Time must be allocated for the children to attach their system part to their card using the glue stick, before moving on. The first child in each group to finish their system shouts out 'System installed!', and receives a prize plus a diploma.

The remaining children are able to finish their game, each choosing a token prize from a box on completion of their system.

PARTY FOOD

PRIZE-WINNING ROSETTES

Blue Mini Fizzers™ or fizzy chew bars
Marie biscuits or Rich Tea™ biscuits
Icing (page 160) – blue
Small foil-covered chocolate coins

1. Shape the ends of the Mini Fizzers™ by cutting diagonally across one tip of each.
2. Place two Mini Fizzers™ in position on the Marie biscuit with the trimmed edges extending as shown, and add a small amount of icing to secure.
3. Use the star nozzle to cover the biscuit with icing.
4. Attach the foil-covered chocolate coin to the centre of the rosette.

BB GRADUATES (BACHELOR OF BISCUITS)

Easy Biscuits (page 161)
Gingerbread 'lady' cookie cutter
Icing (page 160) – blue, and small quantities of yellow and red for the hair and facial features
Silver balls
Liquorice Allsorts™
Liquorice strap

1. Prepare the biscuit dough as per the recipe.
2. Use the lady cookie cutter (so that the gown is depicted) to cut out the biscuits and bake as directed. Leave to cool completely.
3. Use the star nozzle and blue icing to outline the gown with stars. Pipe a row of stars down the centre front and attach silver balls for buttons.
4. Use the yellow icing, star nozzle and the pull-out method to add hair.
5. Place the Liquorice Allsorts™ square in position for the mortarboard.
6. Make the tassel from a thin strip of liquorice. Use a sharp knife to slit one end and attach the opposite end to the centre of the mortarboard, securing with a blob of icing. Add a silver ball as shown.
7. Attach two silver balls with icing for the eyes and pipe a red mouth with the writing nozzle.

CAPPED CUPCAKES

Party Cupcakes (page 161)
Gold foil cookie cups (baking cases)
Icing (page 160) – white
Black Liquorice Allsorts™ square
Ribbon – 2 x 40 mm lengths per treat
Gold balls
Apricot sweets
Red non-toxic food colouring pen for the mouth (or use icing if preferred)
Small star-shaped sweets

1. Bake the cupcakes in the foil cookie cups as directed and leave to cool completely before coating with icing.
2. Make a small slit in the black Liquorice Allsorts™ layer (the mortarboard) and insert two short lengths of ribbon. Secure with a star of icing and top with a gold ball.
3. Place an apricot sweet on the cupcake and attach the mortarboard with a small dab of icing.
4. Using the writing nozzle, add two small blobs of icing to the face and attach gold balls for the eyes.
5. Make a big smiley mouth with the red colouring pen or use the writing nozzle and pipe on the mouth.
6. Attach a star sweet to the cupcake.

SWEET SUCCESS!

Royal blue and/or red ribbons –
about 500 mm long x 10 mm wide – per treat
Ready-made mini swiss rolls

1. Tie a ribbon around each swiss roll to resemble a diploma.
2. Arrange on an attractive serving platter.

A HAPPY BIRTHDAY GRADUATE

1½ x Basic Cake (page 160) – one x 300 x 240 mm cake; one x 200 mm round cake
Icing (page 160) – flesh-coloured, black, red, blue, yellow
Firm cardboard
2 x googly eyes
2 x liquorice strips
1 x mini marshmallow
Sugar paste
Red food colouring
Red flat round sweet

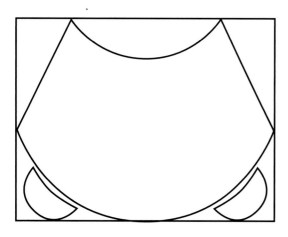
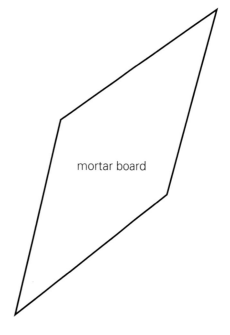

mortar board

1. Bake the cakes as per the recipe and leave to cool completely.
2. Refer to the cutting guide above for the gown and ears and cut these from the rectangular cake.
3. Place the head in position above the gown.
4. Attach an ear to either side of the head with icing.
5. Coat the face and ears with flesh-coloured icing and use a toothpick to define the ear holes.
6. Outline a tie with a toothpick and coat the surrounding gown with black icing. Use the star nozzle to enhance the outline. Decorate the tie with red and blue stripes iced with the star nozzle.
7. To make the mortarboard, enlarge the template provided by about 50 per cent and trace it onto the cardboard. Cut out. Coat one side lightly with black icing and place in position on the head. Use the star nozzle to cover the mortarboard with stars.
8. Attach the eyes and use liquorice strips for the eyebrows. Cut the mini marshmallow in half, coat with flesh-coloured icing and place in position for the nose. Use a toothpick to outline the mouth and define with red icing and the writing nozzle. Fill in the broader portion with stars.
9. The hair is created with yellow icing and the star nozzle. Use the pull-out motion.
10. Colour the sugar paste with the red food colouring and roll into a cord, leaving a slightly thickened section at one end to be cut to resemble a tassel. Attach the other end to the centre of the mortarboard with a dab of icing. Cover with a flat round sweet.

* If a female graduate is preferred, alter by extending the length of the hair strands. Instead of the tie, fill that section with white stars for a blouse and use three or more sweets, depending on preferred size, for buttons. Use a toothpick to outline a round collar at the neck and ice to match the centre section of the blouse.

Setting the Scene

Witness the delight as your guests are transformed into
aspiring ballerinas in twirls of tulle!

* Identify the party venue by attaching a huge pink tulle bow to the front gate. A bunch of pink and white balloons, tied together with pink and white trailing ribbon, may also be included.

* Make pink cardboard cutouts of ballet shoes (see template, page 163) and use them to lay a trail leading from the front gate to the party area.

* Hang a pink tulle curtain in the doorway and use pink bows as tiebacks.

* Use a strip of tulle to make a tutu for a laundry basket to serve as a receptacle for presents.

* Cover the party table with a white tablecloth and pink tulle overlay. Sprinkle with pink confetti and short twirls of pink and white curling ribbon. Scatter pink petals on the table and on the floor.

* Create a canopy above the party table with twisted pink and white streamers draped from the centre of the ceiling to the outer edges. Tie bunches of pink and white balloons together with pink and white curling ribbon and attach to the corners of the ceiling.

* Place a few pink and white sweets on a circle of pink tulle and include a small note on pink paper that says 'Thank you for making my day special'. Gather up and tie the tulle with pink curling ribbon. Suspend these sweet bundles on fishing line from the ceiling above the table at varying heights, and hand one to each guest at the end of the party.

* Line the walls in the party area with lengths of pink tulle and embellish with pink and white balloons and pink and white ribbons.

* Hang bundles of pink and white balloons throughout the house.

Recommended age group: 6-10

Ballet

Invitations

YOU WILL NEED (PER INVITATION):
Ballet shoe template (page 163)
Pencil
White cardboard
Scissors
Pink board paper
Craft knife
Pink notepaper
Pen
Craft glue
Stapler
2 x strips of pink ribbon, each 150 mm long
Small pink bow
Prestik® or Blu-tac™ or adhesive tape

1. Enlarge the template so that the shoe is 180 mm in length. Trace it onto the cardboard and cut out.
2. Duplicate the shape on the pink board paper, this time cutting out the inner section with a craft knife.
3. Duplicate the shape again, this time on the notepaper, and cut out the shape.
4. Write the invitation details (see Suggested Wording) on the notepaper. Glue it underneath the white cardboard sole section. Include the guest's name.
5. Staple one end of each ribbon under the shoe.
6. Glue the pink upper shoe to the sole, covering the stapled ribbon. Glue the bow to the shoe.
7. Cross the ribbon strands over the top of the shoe and attach to the underside, securing with Prestik® or adhesive tape.

SUGGESTED WORDING
Pirouette over to (child's name)'s birthday party on (date)
Dance studio: (address)
Curtain rises: (time party starts)
Final curtsey: (time party ends)
RSVP: The choreographer at (phone number) by (date)
Dress: Tutu!

Treat Bags

YOU WILL NEED (PER BAG):
1 x clean 2-litre soft drink bottle
Craft knife
Paper punch
Needle and pink thread
1 x strip of pink tulle, 140 cm long x 15 cm wide
Prestik® or Blu-tac™
Craft glue
1 x 300 mm-long pink pipe cleaner
Pink board paper
Glitter pen
Pink curling ribbon

1. Cut the top section from the bottle and discard. Punch two holes opposite each other about 1 cm below the rim of the bottle.
2. Run sewing stitches along the upper edge of the length of the tulle and pull to gather so that it fits around the rim of the bottle. Knot the thread and hold the tutu in place with a small dab of Prestik®. Apply dots of craft glue at intervals around the edge to secure the tutu.
3. Insert the ends of the pipe cleaner through the tulle and punched holes to make the handle. Turn up the ends to secure.
4. Write the guest's name on the board paper with the glitter pen. Punch a hole in one corner and attach it to the handle with curling ribbon.

Games and Activities

Apart from the ideas provided below, you may enlist the assistance of a teenager who takes ballet, to guide the children through some basic ballet movements.

Ballet Relay

Have guests sign their shoes at the end of the party as a memento for the birthday child.

YOU WILL NEED:
1 x ballet shoe template (page 163)
Pencil
Poster – one per team
Pink board paper
Scissors
Prestik® or Blu-tac™

Use the template and a pencil to trace outlines of ballet shoes all over the poster, ensuring that you have sufficient outlines for each child per team. Trace the same number of shoes on the pink paper and cut them out. Attach a blob of Prestik® to the underside of each ballet shoe.

Divide the children into two or more teams and have them stand in line, one behind the other. Place the posters at a predetermined distance from the teams.

Hand a ballet shoe to each child. On starter's orders, the first child in each team must run on tiptoe to the appropriate poster and attach her shoe to an outline. She must then twirl around, curtsey, and return to her team, again running on tiptoe. She 'tags' the next child, who repeats the process. The game continues until all the children have had a turn. The first team to finish receives a prize, the rest receive tokens.

Pass the Ballet Shoe

YOU WILL NEED:
1 x ballet shoe
Music

Have the children sit in a circle and pass the shoe from one to the other while the music plays. When the music stops, the child holding the shoe is out. Play continues in the same manner until one child remains. The winner receives a prize, the rest receive tokens.

Do This! Do That!

Play this game using ballet moves, such as: Twirl; Leap; Curtsey; First position; Second position; Star jump; Walk on Tiptoes, and so on.

Have the children follow instructions on the 'Do this!' command. When the 'Do that!' command is given, the children have to remain motionless. Any child who moves is out. If the children are mastering the format, lengthen the pauses after the 'Do that' command while you examine the group for movement – you are sure to eliminate a few twitchy participants! The game continues until there is a winner, who receives a prize. The rest receive tokens.

Prize Leap

YOU WILL NEED:
Cardboard ballet shoes with numbers written on them (use the template on page 163 to trace and cut out the design)
Prestik® or Blu-tac™
Music
1 x box containing number cards
1 x container holding a prize for each child

Fix the numbered shoes to the floor of the party area with Prestik®, placing them at intervals all about the room so that there is sufficient space for movement between each one.

When the music starts, instruct the children to leap like ballerinas, from shoe to shoe, stepping on each as they go. When the music stops the children have to stand on the shoe nearest to them. A number card is pulled from the box and called out, and the child standing on that number leaves the game and chooses a prize from the other container. That particular numbered shoe and card are then removed and the game continues in the same manner until all the children have chosen a prize.

Party Food

Prima Ballerina

Wafer biscuits
Icing (page 160) – white, pink, yellow
White chocolate discs
Candy sticks
Pink and/or silver balls
Red powdered food colouring
Fine paintbrush

1. Coat the wafer biscuits with white icing.
2. Place a chocolate disc in position for the head.
3. Pipe three pink stars below the head for the upper body and a double row of pink stars beneath this for the tutu.
4. Cut candy sticks into 20 mm lengths for the arms and 35 mm lengths for the legs. Press into the icing.
5. Pipe a star at the end of each leg for the shoe and top with a pink ball.
6. Use yellow icing to create hair.
7. Dissolve a pinch of food colouring in a drop of water and paint on a mouth using a fine brush.
8. Attach the eyes with a tiny dab of icing and decorate with pink balls as illustrated.

Ballerina's Best Biscuits

Easy Biscuits (page 161)
Ballet shoe template (page 163)
Icing (page 160) – pink
Ribbon, 2 x 90 mm lengths per biscuit
Pink balls

1. Prepare the biscuit dough as per the recipe.
2. Use the template to cut out the biscuits and bake as directed. Leave the biscuits to cool completely before coating with pink icing.
3. Use a toothpick to define the outer section of the shoe.
4. Place the ribbons in position on the icing.
5. Use the star nozzle to decorate the outer section of the shoe, securing the ribbons at the same time by piping over the ends.
6. Decorate each shoe with a pink ball, as shown.

Party Pirouette

Party Cupcakes (page 161)
Icing (page 160) – pink
Gold foil cookie cups
Ballerina figurines
Pink edible glitter
Pink balls

1. Bake the cupcakes in the cookie cups as per the recipe and leave to cool completely.
2. Coat the cupcakes with a swirl of pink icing, and place a ballerina figure in the centre.
3. Decorate with edible glitter and pink balls.

Tiptoe Treats

Sugar paste
Pink food colouring
Pink balls
Wafer cookie cups
Small sweets of choice
Marie biscuits or Rich Tea™ biscuits
Icing (page 160) – white

1. Colour the sugar paste with the pink food colouring and use a ball about the size of a marble for each shoe.
2. Mould the paste into a sausage shape and then hollow out using the back end of a pencil. Attach a pink ball to each shoe and set aside.
3. Fill the cookie cups with sweets. Coat a Marie biscuit with icing and place it, iced side down, over the cookie cup to seal it. Upend so that the Marie biscuit forms the base.
4. Coat the top of the cookie cup with icing and use the star nozzle to pipe a row of stars around the upper edge as well as around the base.
5. Place the ballet shoes on the top as shown, using a dab of icing to stick them together.

Centre Stage Birthday Cake

1 x Basic Cake (page 160) – 300 x 240 mm
Sugar paste – white
Flower-shaped cutter
Icing (page 160) – pink
Star- or flower-shaped mirror
Ballerina figurines
Prestik® or Blu-tac™
Gold balls

1. Bake the cake according to the recipe and leave to cool completely.
2. Roll out the sugar paste to 2–4 mm thick and cut out flowers with the cutter. Set aside to firm. If preferred, use ready-made, store-bought sugar flowers.
3. Coat the cake with pink icing and use the star nozzle to decorate the sides and edges.
4. Place the mirror in position at the centre back of the 'stage' and pipe pink stars around the edge.
5. Attach a ballerina to the mirror using a small piece of Prestik® to secure (conceal with pink sugar paste).
6. Place the remaining ballerinas in position and decorate the cake with the sugar paste flowers. Use the gold balls and pink icing to enhance the flowers.

RECITES

Note: Extra-large eggs (61–68 g) have been used throughout.

BASIC CAKE

Makes 1 x rectangular cake measuring 300 x 240 mm; OR 1 x round cake measuring 280 mm in diameter; OR 2 x round cakes measuring 200 mm in diameter; OR 2 x 200 mm square cakes; OR 3 x large food cans (750 g); OR 1 x 1.5 litre ovenproof pudding bowl and 1 x 0.5 litre ovenproof pudding bowl.

4 eggs
300 g (300 ml) white sugar
2½ cups (625 ml) cake (plain) flour
4 tsp (20 ml) baking powder
a pinch of salt
¾ cup (180 ml) oil
¾ cup (180 ml) water
1 tsp (5 ml) vanilla essence

1. Preheat the oven to 180 °C (350 °F, Gas Mark 4).
2. Beat the eggs, then gradually add the sugar and beat until thick and pale.
3. In a separate bowl, sift the flour, baking powder and salt together.
4. In another bowl, lightly whisk the oil, water and vanilla essence to combine.
5. Gently fold the dry ingredients, alternately with the liquid, into the egg mixture.
6. Depending on your requirements, pour the cake batter into the required greased cake tin(s).
7. Bake for 25–30 minutes. To test whether the cake is baked through, insert a skewer into the centre of the cake. If it comes out clean, the cake is done. Where the cakes are baked in pudding bowls or food cans, the baking times may vary slightly and should be monitored. The 1.5 litre pudding bowl will bake for about 1 hour, whereas the 0.5 litre container will bake for about 25 minutes. The large food cans bake for about the same time as the conventional tins, whereas the smaller tins should be done in 20–25 minutes.
8. Turn out onto a rack to cool completely before icing.

ICING

This recipe is sufficient to ice the basic cake, but for larger cakes, and particularly where the star nozzle is used, the quantity will have to be doubled.

100 g white margarine, at room temperature
2½ cups (625 ml) icing sugar, sifted
± 5 tsp (25 ml) boiling water
½ tsp (2.5 ml) vanilla essence

1. Mix together the margarine and sifted icing sugar.
2. Add the boiling water, a little at a time, and mix until the desired consistency is obtained.
3. Add the vanilla essence.
4. Once the icing has been mixed, it may be coloured by adding powdered colouring, blending in small quantities (about ¼ tsp/ 1 ml) at a time, until the desired shade is obtained. Liquid colouring may be used if preferred, but care should be taken that the consistency does not become too runny.

For chocolate icing
Add 2 Tbsp (30 ml) sifted cocoa powder to the icing sugar and proceed as above.

PARTY CUPCAKES

MAKES ABOUT 20

1½ cups (375 ml) self-raising flour
1 tsp (5 ml) baking powder
a pinch of salt
¾ cup (180 ml) sugar
2 eggs
½ cup (125 ml) oil
½ cup (125 ml) milk
1 tsp (5 ml) vanilla essence

1. Preheat the oven to 180 °C
   (350 °F, Gas Mark 4).
2. Mix the dry ingredients together.
3. Beat the eggs lightly and add the
   oil, milk and vanilla essence.
4. Add the liquid to the dry
   ingredients and mix well.
5. Spoon the mixture into cookie
   cups (baking cases) in a muffin
   tray and bake for 12–15 minutes.
6. Leave to cool before icing

EASY BISCUITS

MAKES ABOUT 24
(DEPENDING ON THE SHAPE)

125 g butter
½ cup (125 ml) castor sugar
1 tsp (5 ml) vanilla essence
1 egg, beaten
2 cups (500 ml) cake (plain) flour
4 Tbsp (60 ml) cornflour
1 tsp (5 ml) baking powder
a pinch of salt

1. Preheat the oven to 180 °C
   (350 °F, Gas Mark 4).
2. Beat together the butter and
   castor sugar until pale.
3. Add the vanilla essence and
   beaten egg.
4. Add the sifted dry ingredients.
   Knead well to form a stiff dough.
5. Roll out on a lightly floured board
   to a thickness of 3–4 mm.
6. Cut into the desired shapes.
7. Bake on a greased baking tray
   for 10–12 minutes until lightly
   browned.
8. Leave to cool completely before
   coating with icing.
9. The dough may be prepared in
   advance and frozen until required
   (will keep for 4–6 weeks).
   Alternatively, bake the biscuits
   in advance and freeze until
   required.

MERINGUES

MAKES ABOUT 36
(DEPENDING ON THE SHAPE)

4 egg whites
a pinch of salt
1½ cups (375 ml) castor sugar

1. Preheat the oven to 100 °C
   (200 °F, Gas Mark ¼).
2. Whisk the egg whites and salt
   until stiff and dry.
3. Gradually add half the sugar and
   whisk until stiff peaks form.
4. Fold in the remaining sugar,
   gently but thoroughly.
5. Spoon about 2 tsp (10 ml) of the
   mixture onto baking sheets lined
   with greaseproof paper, spaced
   about 80 mm apart.
6. Bake for about 45 minutes.
   Switch off the oven, keep the
   door shut, and leave the
   meringues to cool completely,
   preferably overnight.

TEMPLATES

Page 7

Page 29

Pages 7, 10, 43, 57, 66

Pages 13, 14

Page 54

Pages 29, 30

Pages 15, 18

Pages 46, 48

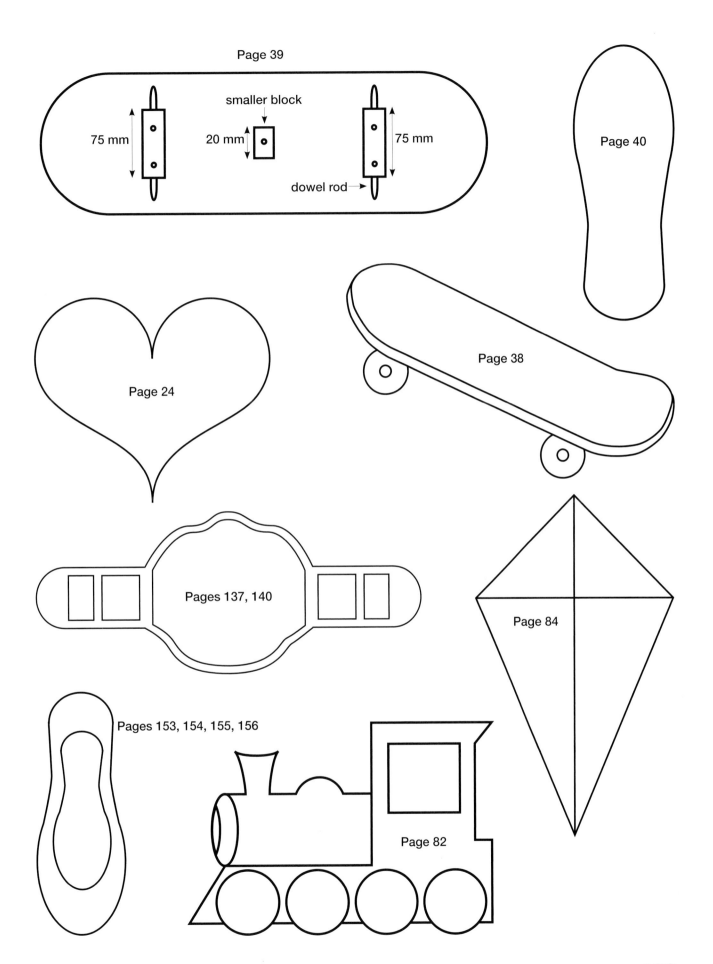

Page 39

smaller block

75 mm

20 mm

75 mm

dowel rod →

Page 40

Page 24

Page 38

Pages 137, 140

Page 84

Pages 153, 154, 155, 156

Page 82

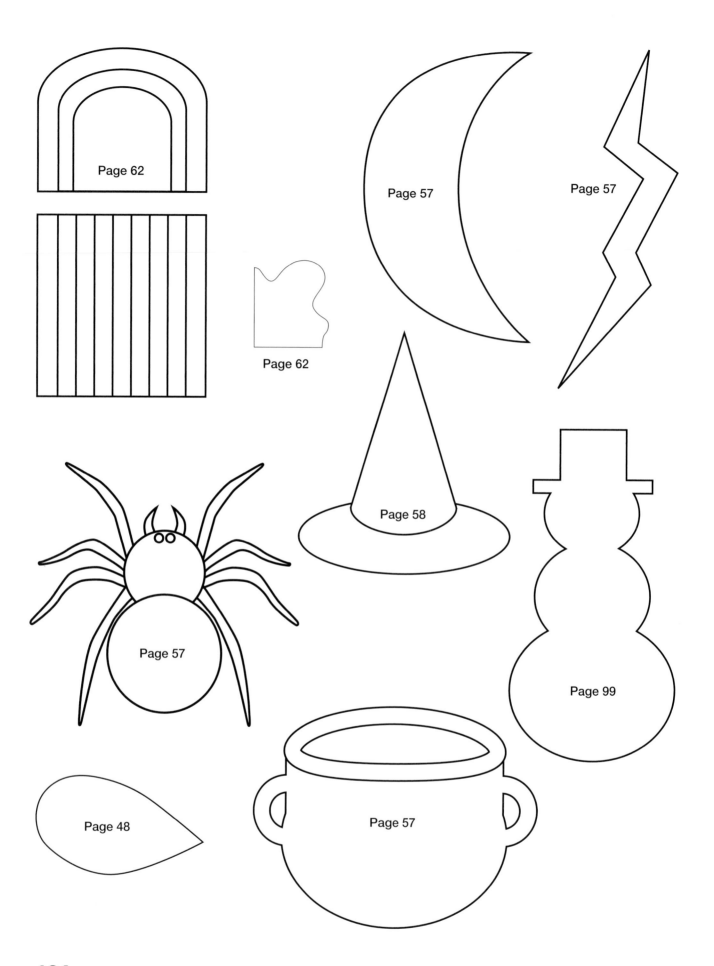

Page 62

Page 62

Page 57

Page 57

Page 58

Page 57

Page 99

Page 48

Page 57

Page 74

Page 124

Page 92

Page 122

Page 132

Page 116

Page 74

Pages 73, 76

STOCKISTS

SOUTH AFRICA

BAKING SUPPLIES
The Baking Tin
- 52 Belvedere Rd, Claremont, Cape Town. Tel: (021) 671 6434.
- 132 Durban Rd, Bellville, Cape Town. Tel: (021) 948 2274.
- Shop 23, Glenwood Village, Cnr Hunt & Moore Rd, Glenwood, Durban. Tel: (031) 202 2224.
- Rochel Rd, Perridgevale, Port Elizabeth. Tel: (041) 363 0271.

Confectionery Extravaganza
82 Dan Pienaar St, Florida Hills, Roodepoort. Tel: (011) 672 4766.

South Bakels
19 Henry van Rooijen St, Bloemfontein. Tel: (051) 432 8446.

P.Q. Products
Unit 1A, Millside Park, 35 Morningside Rd, Ndabeni, Cape Town. Tel: (021) 531 4061.

Garner Wafers and Confectionery
35 Stella Rd, Montague Gardens, Cape Town. Tel: (021) 552 0250.

TOYS/ACCESSORIES
Denson's Party World
120 Voortrekker Rd, Parow, Cape Town. Tel: (021) 930 4882.

Plastics for Africa
3b Montague Drive, Montague Gardens, Cape Town.
Tel: (021) 551 5790.

Plastics Warehouse
26 Northumberland Rd, Bellville, Cape Town. Tel: (021) 948 3042.

The Crazy Store
Branches countrywide.
Head Office Tel: (021) 505 5500.
www.crazystore.co.za

The Excitement Store
Branches countrywide.
www.excitement.co.za

SWEETS/CHOCOLATES
Shoprite
Branches countrywide.
www.shoprite.co.za

Giant Sweet Wholesalers
3 Benbell Ave, Epping 1, Cape Town. Tel: (021) 534 5925.

Sweets from Heaven
Branches countrywide.
www.theheavengroup.com

Jelly Babes
Howard Centre, Pinelands, Cape Town. Tel: (021) 531 2155.

PACKAGING
Merrypak & Print
Packaging Warehouse
- 45 Morningside Rd, Ndabeni, Cape Town. Tel: (021) 531 2244.
- 21 Bridlington Rd, Seaview, Durban. Tel: (031) 465 2719.

CRAFT/FABRIC SUPPLIES
Beads For Africa
111 N1 City Mall, Goodwood, Cape Town. Tel: (021) 595 2845.

Cape Arts and Crafts
Canal Walk, Cape Town.
Tel: (021) 555 3699.

Fabric City Wholesalers
32 Sir Lowry Rd, Cape Town.
Tel: (021) 462 1287.

Arts, Crafts and Hobbies
72 Hibernia St, George.
Tel: (044) 874 1337.

Maridadi Crafts
Shop 4, Centurion Mall, Centurion, Pretoria. Tel: (012) 663 4030.

Crafts from our Heart
Shop 1A, Paige Place, Bamboo Lane, Pinetown. Tel: 082 777 9020.

UNITED KINGDOM
Consult the Yellow Pages for cake decorating and party supplier shops.

Culpitt Ltd (baking supplies)
Jubilee Industrial Estate, Ashington, Northumberland, NE63 8UQ.
Tel: 01670 814545. www.culpitt.com

London Sugarart Centre (baking supplies)
12 Selkirk Rd, London SW17 0ES.
Tel: 020 8767 8558.

Toys R Us (toys, games)
Stores nationwide.
Freepost Nat 3362, Gateshead NE10 8BR. www.toysrus.co.uk

Woolworths (toys, sweets, chocolates)
Stores nationwide.
Tel: 0845 608 1100.
www.woolworths.co.uk

Paperchase (gift bags, ribbons, party boxes)
Stores nationwide.
213–215 Tottenham Court Rd, London W1T 7PS.
www.paperchase.co.uk

Hobbycraft (craft supplies)
Stores nationwide.
7 Enterprise Way, Aviation Park, Bournemouth International Airport, Christchurch, Dorset BH23 6HG.
Tel: 01202 596100.
www.hobbycraft.co.uk

John Lewis (fabrics, ribbons from haberdashery department)
Contact head office for stores.
Oxford St, London W1A 1EX.
www.johnlewis.com

INDEX